To Dad
with love from
Christine
x x

By the same Author

The Thin Yellow Line
The Durham Light Infantry
See How They Ran
Fetch Felix
Against the Assegai
Storm of Steel
Bayonets in the Sun

THE LONG WAY ROUND

THE LONG WAY ROUND

An Escape Through Occupied France

by

WILLIAM MOORE

Leo Cooper
in association with
Secker and Warburg

First published in Great Britain in 1986 by
Leo Cooper in Association with Secker and Warburg Ltd
54 Poland Street London W1V 3DF
Copyright © William Moore 1986

ISBN: 0-436-28463-4

Printed in Great Britain by
Richard Clay (The Chaucer Press) Ltd,
Bungay, Suffolk

Contents

	Introduction	ix
Chapter I	All on a Summer's Day	1
Chapter II	Of Kilts and Lice	10
Chapter III	Oh, to be in Shanghai	17
Chapter IV	Serious Officers All	23
Chapter V	Jimmy Stepforit	31
Chapter VI	One More River	39
Chapter VII	Ghost Patrol	47
Chapter VIII	The Nun's Tale	56
Chapter IX	Hutch of Happiness	63
Chapter X	Spandaus for a Saint	70
Chapter XI	*'Brigitte est là . . .'*	77
Chapter XII	*'Verboten, verboten . . .'*	83
Chapter XIII	Love and Blackmail	91
Chapter XIV	Jodhpurs Princess	99
Chapter XV	*'Quoi, Alors, Comment!'*	107
Chapter XVI	Afternoon Matinée	116
Chapter XVII	Over the Border	125
Chapter XVIII	Beau Chumps	132
Chapter XIX	Bad Girls Make Good	138
Chapter XX	Hitler's Toothache	145
Chapter XXI	*'Arriba Churchill!'*	151
Chapter XXII	A Sergeant's Pride	156
Chapter XXIII	No Liver, no Chips	161

Contents

Chapter XXIV   The Reckoning   171

Chapter XXV   Just Call Me 'Sir'   175

Appendix A   Order of Battle of the
     51st Highland Division   180

Appendix B   *Services Speciaux*   181

Introduction

Escape and evasion exercises are part of standard military training today. No good soldier expects to end up 'in the bag' but it is as well to be prepared for all eventualities.

Things have changed drastically since mediaeval times when the rich were ransomed and archers or common soldiers were knocked on the head if they did not switch sides quickly enough. Prisoners were often exchanged during the eighteenth and nineteenth centuries, though there was an unpleasant alteration in tradition when, during the American Civil War, some smart Yankee calculated that the trade was of more benefit to the South.

In the First World War repatriation was restricted to the seriously ill and disabled. Fit officers and men were held for 'the duration'. A number of 'evasions' were successful in 1914, during the brief period of mobile warfare, and later some daring escapes were made from prison camps. It was not considered essential, however, to make a serious study of the experience available. Twenty or more years later the game had to be learned from the beginning as far as the British were concerned. In France there was the *Société des Evades (1914–18)* which set up an undercover relief organization in 1940, sending civilian clothes to prisoners in the Occupied Zone and establishing lines of escape to Vichy France.

In 1940 most of Western Europe was held in subjection by the Nazis and their collaborators. The Germans held one and a half million French PoWs alone. Thousands of civilians were placed in some sort of custody.

As the war dragged on the Allied military authorities placed an increasingly high priority on the recovery of trained men, particularly

air crew, stranded in enemy territory. Fliers were equipped with concealed compasses, scarves became maps, caps contained currency.
Throughout Europe networks evolved to help escapers reach some point
from which they could be picked up and returned home. Some routes,
such as the Var Line on the North Breton coast and the Pat Line
through Marseilles, were highly efficient. A housewife who sheltered an
airman for the night in the Suisse Normande met him again a few weeks
later. He had been back to Britain, rejoined his squadron and been shot
down again.

What makes the journey of a second-lieutenant and seven men of the
Seaforth Highlanders remarkable is that, when they decided to make
their way home the long way round from the battlefield of St Valery-en-
Caux in June, 1940, none of the aids which came into being later had
been introduced. Indeed their adventures actually began before Pétain
had asked for an armistice.

The men were in uniform and armed. Their leader, Richard Broad,
was the only one who spoke enough French to make himself understood.
His exploits, including his subsequent experiences with the Special
Operations Executive in Madagascar and his involvement in airborne
and commando operations, have been dealt with in a biographical book
(*A Talent to Survive* by Rex Woods, published by William Kimber). This
study concentrates on the events and people involved in the journey
which began at St Valery in June, 1940, and ended in London in May,
1941.

Individuals had made it home before them. A few groups made the
journey afterwards, but not as the remnants of a single battalion. The
achievement of the handful of Seaforths remains unique. They did not
indulge in heroics. They blew up no installations, knifed no sentries. But
their very ability to exist for a long period in the midst of the heavily
guarded coastal zone – the *zone cotière interdit* – was an inspiration to all
who came to know about it. Their incredible excursion to Paris pro-
foundly affected those who helped them. Broad and the Jocks with him
brought back proof that the embryo French Resistance movement
meant business.

Many of the French who played a part in this story were involved in
grimmer events afterwards, but all those who survived recall with
something akin to affection the details of *l'affaire Broad* or the passage of
'Snow White and the Seven Dwarfs' as they were known.

Participants in those events of 1940/41 are scattered. The trail led
from a village in the pine forests south of Bordeaux to a farmhouse on

the outskirts of Cambrai. The inhabitants of elegant Paris flats, no-nonsense farmhouses and simple cottages made fascinating contributions. There were sad moments – the lady in the Rue aux Chats had died some time previously; a once charming villa which had been a haven for the Seaforths stood empty and forlorn, a large tree uprooted by a storm lying in the neglected garden.

Naturally the people had changed. For example, the little nun who played such an important role had become a mother superior, but she still tended the sick and needy from a pleasant convent house incongruously sited opposite the walls of Dieppe's forbidding prison.

One thing had not altered. There was no shortage of goodwill, kindness, consideration or understanding. That France and Britain do not always see eye to eye is well known, but there is a widespread warmth of feeling for the British in France which must not be allowed to cool. If this book helps even a little way in that direction it will have been worth while.

I would like to express my gratitude to Richard Broad for putting all his papers at my disposal and for his advice and friendship, and to his wife Joan for joining in the project so enthusiastically; to George Dodd who saw it all through the eyes of a private soldier; and to the following French men and women (in the order in which they entered the affair): Monsieur Roland Mourot; Monsieur and Madame Edmond Bailleul; Mère Marie-Gabriel (of the Franciscan Order); Madame Nicole Bouchet de Fareins; Madame 'Francette' Drin; Monsieur Gustav Lust; Madame Irma Cornière; Madame Madeleine Morin; Monsieur Jacques Robert; Monsieur André Postel-Vinay; Colonel Léon Simoneau and Comte Pierre de Francqueville. I am also grateful to the Comtesse d'Harcourt, whose husband, the late Comte Pierre d'Harcourt, played such a vital part, for her help. Finally I must acknowledge my wife's considerable contribution to helping me attain my goal.

Rouville la Bigot
1985

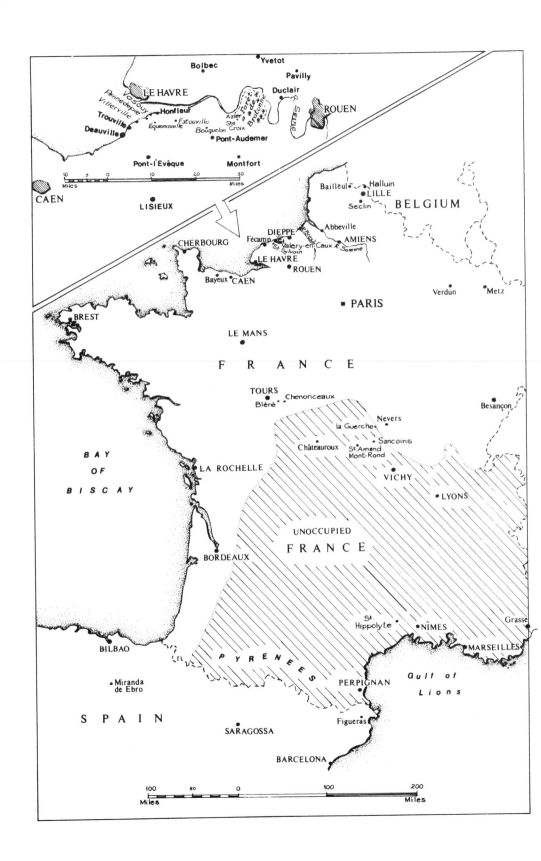

I

All on a Summer's Day

As far as Private Dodd was concerned Tuesday had started indifferently, deteriorated rapidly and was showing every sign of getting worse. He was dirty, famished and desperately tired. He tried to ease the suffering of the wounded Jocks crammed in the back of his 15 cwt by changing down as they bumped over the rutted track leading out of the wood, but the ground was baked hard. The jolting continued.

Private Dodd was not sorry to be leaving the wood. When 'D' Company had occupied it that morning he had parked and camouflaged his vehicle and then sweated with the others to dig a large hole. This they had roofed over with tree trunks and branches which they had covered with earth and turf to make a flimsy dugout. Around them stretched the expanse of scrub dotted with large stumps and sundry beeches and oaks.

At the edge of the timber, the rifle platoons – or what remained of them – had scratched similar positions. Occasional bursts of rifle and Bren fire had been punctuated by the piercing crack of an anti-tank rifle.

Dodd had seen nothing of the enemy, whose bullets were tearing through the branches overhead, showering him with leaves and splinters. After a slow start the Germans had warmed to their work and, as the sun burned off the heat haze, small-calibre, high-velocity shells had come hissing into the area. Reports said the Panzers were multiplying, though they were still keeping a respectable distance.

As the German fire increased so did the stream of wounded seeking shelter. The dugout overflowed with men, some groaning, others white-

faced and silent. There were few stretchers and scarcely any field
dressings. A sergeant-major and half a dozen men from an English
county Territorial regiment began to show signs of hysteria. Smoke
from burning brushwood drifted across the scene. It was a relief to get
an order.

'Come on, driver. Let's get some of these wounded chaps out of
here.'

Lieutenant Laidlaw, who had either joined as a stray or been
posted in as a reinforcement, spoke with a jauntiness that belied his
lined face. 'They'll be better off with the MO. We can't do much for
them here.'

Dodd agreed heartily and wasted no time in stripping the camouflage
off his vehicle.

'Battalion HQ, sir?'

'That's right.'

Dodd grimaced and tried to concentrate.

'Do you know the way, sir?'

'I think so. Don't you?'

Dodd looked doubtful.

'Somewhere over there, perhaps.'

He had an idea that not far from St Valery Headquarters and 'C'
Company had taken a road to the left.

The officer followed Dodd's outstretched arm.

'That's where they should be all right. Let's see if we can find
them.'

Some of the wounded were too ill to move but eight were heaved or
helped into the back of the truck. As the tailboard was secured one of
them leaned over and said hoarsely, 'At least we know something the
ruddy folks at home don't know, Doddy!'

'What's that?'

'We know what Hell's like!'

The joker fell back wheezing at his own wit.

Army vehicle Z372122 had behaved impeccably since it had been
driven out of Maryhill Barracks nine months earlier. Between the
machine and Private Dodd there was complete rapport. Other people's
transport might break down, shed bits, make unseemly noises and
belch oily smoke from their exhausts. Some even contrived to get in the
way of bombs and shells. Not 22. Now the magic worked again.

The moment they reached the cart track leading out of the shot-torn wood the racket diminished. In the open cab Dodd could now feel rather than hear heavy explosions, probably in the port area, but no one seemed to be interested in a solitary lorry. They crossed a metalled road and saw some German tanks in the distance, but these either ignored the fugitives or the crews were looking elsewhere. The wood was not yet surrounded but it was only a matter of time. Shortly afterwards, directed partly by Lieutenant Laidlaw who sat by his side with a rough sketch map, partly by his own hunch and under 22's benign influence, they made their way to the headquarters of the 2nd Battalion, the Seaforth Highlanders.

Dodd could not decide whether it was an outsize farm or a stunted village. Typical Norman banks-cum-hedges, each about 400 yards long, formed three sides of a rough square which was blocked at one end by another scrubby wood. Within this enclosure stood four or five buildings, log piles and manure heaps. Just inside the ungated gap which led into this area was a fine old barn criss-crossed with dark oak beams, the lath and plaster walls recently lime-washed. Inside this picture-postcard setting the Medical Officer had established his aid post. Private Dodd helped unload some of the wounded, tactfully avoiding the end of the barn which had been turned into a mortuary. Then he went in search of orders. Shouldn't he head back to 'D' Company? They might need him.

The Regimental Sergeant-Major * was adamant that he would never make it. 'I don't think there can be many left up there by now . . . not alive anyway. You just stay by your lorry, Dodd. We'll let you know if you're wanted. In the mean time you know how to use that.'

He tapped the crossed-rifles insignia on Private Dodd's sleeve.

'Keep your weapon with you. You're going to need it. Not much seems to be going right today.'

Not much was going right either for Mr Winston Churchill who, like Private Dodd, was also in France on 11 June, 1940, having flown to an airfield near Orleans in a Flamingo passenger plane escorted by twelve fighters. Regardless of the risk of interception by roving enemy aircraft, or even of simple engine failure, Churchill was accompanied by several key figures including Mr Anthony Eden, Secretary of State for War, General Sir John Dill, Chief of the Imperial General Staff, and Major-General 'Pug' Ismay, head of the military section of the War Cabinet Secretariat.

* RSM John Keil.

The previous day the French Government had left Paris.

Near the town of Briare, in a large modern red-brick villa bearing the name 'Lily of the Valley Château', the British visitors were given tea before being addressed by General Maxime Weygand, the 73-year-old Supreme Commander of the Allied armies. In the presence of Monsieur Paul Reynaud, the French premier, they listened to the harrowing tale of a battle which had raged non-stop for six days and had left Weygand without any reserves – not a single battalion. The troops were exhausted. The combination of German bombers and tanks was devastating. There was nothing to prevent the enemy entering Paris, which had been declared an open city.

'We are fighting on our last line and it has been breached.' Weygand's shrill voice rose a tone higher. 'I am helpless. I cannot intervene. I have no reserves. This is the break-up.'

This from the man who had read out the Armistice terms to the Germans in the railway carriage at Compiègne in 1918, the man who had been Chief of Staff to Marshal Foch, the architect of victory. The uniform was immaculate as ever, the ex-cavalryman's topboots still gleamed, the hard, almost Asiatic face remained set, but there was no hope to be found in the eyes.

Then Marshal Pétain spoke, Pétain whom Reynaud had brought into the Cabinet as his deputy three weeks earlier as a symbolic gesture. At 84 the hero of Verdun, the past-master of the counter-offensive, had followed the account with difficulty because of deafness . . . though he probably knew enough already. The translucent pallor of the very old was exaggerated by a dark civilian suit. His moustache no longer flowed, the blue eyes no longer pierced. He was sure General Weygand's assessment of the situation was correct. When Churchill recalled the dark days of 1918, he said unemotionally, 'In those days there were sixty British divisions in the line.'

There was no answer to that. At that moment parts of the 1st Armoured Division were still in action, but all that remained of the original British Expeditionary Force's first-line infantry formations was the battered 51st Highland Division. That, reduced to two brigades because the remnants of the third had been sent to protect Le Havre, was trapped with the French IXth Corps at the little port of St Valery-en-Caux. Its predicament was very much in the mind of Churchill and his colleagues but they avoided direct reference to it at Briare. It had become a touchy subject.

On 4 June Major-General Victor Fortune, the 57-year-old commander of the 51st, had directed a promising Anglo-French attack against the German bridgehead over the Somme at Abbeville. Stout opposition, lack of reserves and a desire to preserve the surviving French armour for further action, prevented the success being exploited. The next day dive bombers and tanks spearheaded a major offensive which drove the Scots and the neighbouring French division back to the line of the River Bresle. On Weygand's express orders they hung on there. Warnings that they would be cut off in the Havre peninsula were ignored until too late. The Germans entered Rouen, the bridges were blown and there was no means of crossing the Seine. Not without reason the British felt that if Fortune had been allowed to retire on Rouen earlier, his men might have escaped. But by 9 June the trap was sprung.

Yet Weygand would accept no criticism of himself. On the 6th he had complained that Fortune had fallen back without orders. His behaviour had been intolerable. He did not understand the seriousness of the struggle and his men were 'fighting indifferently'. He suggested that the General would be better named 'Misfortune'. Some French officers felt that he ought to be court-martialled.

By the time of the Briare Conference, however, the fate of a single division was of relatively minor importance. Grave matters of state took precedence. The British strained every nerve to persuade the French to continue the struggle from their colonies if the Battle of France was lost. Most of the French present – the junior General de Gaulle being an exception – were intent on making their ally realize that a request for an armistice was essential. Repeatedly from Weygand came the doleful phrase: 'We are at the last quarter of an hour.'

For all too many Jocks the last quarter of an hour had come and gone. As the afternoon of the 11th wore on the tanks tightened the ring around the 2nd Seaforths. From beyond the range of the defenders' weapons they raked the area with machine guns and with 20-millimetre and 37-millimetre shells. The Highlanders, unable to knock out the armour, waited under cover for the enemy infantry to appear. Inevitably the streams of tracer and incendiary started fires and with a roar the aid post roof burst into flames.

The scene that followed convinced Private Dodd that his hopes of reaching the beaches and Navy were slim indeed. Medical orderlies lay dead among the corpses of the men they had tended. The Medical Officer, Lieutenant McKillop, was propped outside the barn with tourniquets round his mangled legs in a vain attempt to stop him bleeding to death, while soldiers brought him a stream of wounded. As he lay dying, he displayed remarkable bravery by trying to tell others how to bandage the wounded.*

The RSM appeared through the smoke and told Dodd not to worry about the wounded. He said there was a Jerry sniper over by a corner, shooting at anything that moved.

Private Dodd followed the RSM's glance. After a few seconds a helmeted figure appeared round the end of a barn and fired at troops carrying men from the blazing building.

Dodd climbed into the back of 22, spread himself on the blood-stained floor and adjusted his sights to 300 yards. While he was doing so the German took another pot shot. When he reappeared Dodd's bullet hit him in the head, hurling him backwards. A weapon flew into the air. Seconds later a motor-cycle combination, the side-car empty, gathered speed as it passed across the ungated entrance to the area. Dodd fired again. The machine crashed into a tree and began to burn, the rider slumped across the handlebars.

Smoke from blazing buildings now hindered the Germans, who decided against risking their tanks in the blinding clouds and contented themselves with long-range fire.

Towards evening the tanks withdrew to refuel and replenish their ammunition, leaving infantry to contain the position. A comparative fall in the noise level was broken at 9 o'clock when a violent bombardment fell on St Valery. Major-General Erwin Rommel, commanding the 7th Panzer Division, had ordered every gun under his command to blast the northern end of the town. Field guns, anti-aircraft guns, anti-tank guns, mortars and heavies opened up a concentrated and rapid fire. The flickering dull red glow which had tinted the smoke clouds over the port grew brighter and spread.

Private Dodd and the other Jocks looked at one another uneasily, thinking the same thing. The Germans had been shelling the town as they left that morning and had already set the Town Hall and the Post Office ablaze. This new blasting was ten times worse. Were they, because of their presence earlier, the cause of the devastation?

Dense showers of sparks shot skywards over St Valery.

Dodd dozed through the night, rifle in hand. Until the beginning of

* After the war the then Colonel Broad found McKillop's grave, simply inscribed 'Lieutenant RAMC – unknown'. He had this altered.

May he had been unable to take the war seriously. Stuck on the Belgian border without a German in sight, the most difficult thing had been to keep warm. The only threat was from the Military Police when stealing coal. This he had done with a small band of desperadoes who had crossed the Albert canal, loaded a raft with the contents of a coal yard and floated their booty across to where he was waiting with his lorry. That's what came of putting good soldiers in a cinema hall with one bucket of fuel a night for a stove built to take five hundredweight.

Only when they were switched to the Saar front, with a real enemy opposed to them, did he realize that things were changing. As the transport column drew near the front a far-off rumbling began. It reached a frightening crescendo and thundered over them to fade away in the distance. Vivid flashes and sheet lightning accompanied the noise, which, in minutes, was repeated with a slight change in tone but not in volume. The Maginot and Siegfried Lines were bellowing ritual defiance, fire rippling from a succession of forts on one side and being answered in the same way from the other.

Dodd could make little sense of the events that followed the opening of the German blitzkrieg on 10 May. The battalion seemed to move this way and that for ten days before being pulled out of the area and concentrated near Verdun. Then the infantry were sent off by train and the rumour went round that they were going to defend Paris. The idea appealed to Dodd but he was sorry that the move interrupted a promising romance with a girl he had met in a café in Metz. Hopes of keeping his promise to return to see her dwindled rapidly as the convoy was engulfed by the chaos on the roads.

A week passed before they picked up the battalion again – in the bomb-cratered station yard at Rouen. The troops reckoned the train had been almost to the south of France before coming north again.

Various adventures befell Dodd in the fighting around Abbeville and the subsequent retreat. For a start he got lost while carrying the company cook and all his paraphernalia. They drove into a village square full of German transport, but turned and fled without the loss of a saucepan. In deserted hamlets they helped themselves to chickens which they cooked gipsy fashion, unplucked in clay, because they did not want to leave any evidence. Eventually Dodd and his culinary cargo were reorientated by a vigilant Royal Military Police officer who intercepted the vehicle en route for Paris which they were certain was still the battalion's destination. A motor-cyclist guided them to a rendez-vous where, to Dodd's surprise, a familiar face greeted him. The

Redcap directing the traffic had been a regular customer at the same fish and chip shop before he joined up. He agreed to come and see Dodd when he came off duty.

Dodd glanced backed as he turned into a gate about a hundred yards further on. For a second the familiar figure waving on the traffic was impressed on his vision. In the same second a pillar of smoke and flame engulfed it.

The bomb must have been a freak from a stick that landed some distance away. There were no others and Dodd went back to the spot as soon as he had parked. In the smoking blackened hole, about fifteen feet across, there was nothing to indicate a human being had ever occupied the spot; not a scrap of body tissue, not a fragment of cloth, webbing or leather.

When dawn broke over St Valery on 12 June Dodd knew that anything which arrived from Hitler that day was going to be unpleasant. From the comings and goings of the night he could glean little. He was a 'D' Company man among strangers. He tried to find the acting transport officer – the original MTO had been killed by a strafing Messerschmitt – but was told he had last been seen heading for St Valery with a Bren gunner perched in the cab of the lorry.

Only by chance did Dodd learn that all vehicles and equipment which might be of value to the enemy were to be destroyed. After that the troops could decide for themselves whether to give up or make a break for it. Someone said the French had already surrendered, though gunfire could still be heard from the direction of the coast.

Army vehicle Z372122 was despatched swiftly as befitted an old and trusted servant. It had carried guns and girls, rations and riflemen and crates of beer galore. Dodd opened the bonnet and took a last look at the dependable engine before crashing down a 12-pound hammer with all his might. Then he slashed the tyres. There was no easy way out now.

He joined a group of hollow-eyed Jocks. He said nothing because they were older men, reservists who had 'done their seven' and been recalled to the Colours. Some wore campaign ribbons. Worn out by days of marching and fighting, their conversation was thick and dis-jointed, but the drift began to come through. . . . They had been pushed to their limit . . . let down by the French . . . everyone else had cleared off. Two of them agreed that for them it was all over.

Dodd wondered whether he had heard correctly. These men were

Regulars, men he had looked up to. And he knew they could fight – an ammunition check had shown them to have only five rounds per man left. They just couldn't give up like that. He backed away in disgust and walked over to a ditch, trying to think. Finally he decided to crawl along it.

The ditch muffled the sound of battle but he could hear plenty of creaking and rattling from tanks on the road. At intervals he peered out, searching for a friendly face. Sometimes he crawled, rifle before him. Sometimes he just lay there. Then, on one of his periodic surfacings, he saw Drayton, whom he recognized by the tilt of his Balmoral.

If there was something different about Drayton at that moment it was that his usual happy-go-lucky manner had vanished and he was trying – one could not say more – to behave furtively. He was peering giraffe-like from a field of waist-high corn at a German tank which had just clattered past at full speed, hatches down.

In a twinkling he had submerged in the ripening grain. In another twinkling Dodd crossed the road and dived after him.

II

Of Kilts and Lice

The smoke from the locomotive, which had rolled over the stark factories and grimy towns of the industrial North, was whipped away in the clean air of the Border country. Then the Highlands began and Dodd started to speculate on the welcome he would receive. Was it really such a good idea for a Cheshire country lad to plunge into a closed society dominated by alien Scots? He decided to make the most of the fact that he had relatives in Glasgow and play down his grandfather's long service in the Cheshire Yeomanry.

Young Dodd had gone to some lengths to enlist. His reason, in part, was to get away from people who kept on telling him to be careful. As a boy he had been run over by a coal lorry and had endured twenty-one operations in twenty-two days at the hands of a family doctor called Okel (GPs did that sort of thing in the 30s). Since then he had been considered 'delicate' and treated as such. The Army offered an escape from the mollycoddlers.

In choosing the Seaforth Highlanders he was influenced greatly by his father. Dodd senior had served as a gunner in the Great War and, though from Winsford, Cheshire, had sung the praises of the Scottish regiment ever since he had seen it in action on the Western Front. Despite his father's blessing, Dodd still had a problem as he was only seventeen. To get round it he joined the local Territorial Army unit, the 7th Cheshires, and took advantage of a scheme which encouraged transfers to regular service. In this way, he believed, he would not be asked for his birth certificate at the recruiting office. Whether this subterfuge was necessary is questionable.

Anyway there was no hitch when, on 20 April, 1938, George William Dodd signed the blue paper that committed him to serve seven years with the Colours and five on the Reserve.

The journey began in the noisy, dark cave of Crewe station. Self-consciously he and another recruit presented their travel warrants at the ticket office and sought seats together. Both were suffering from second thoughts by the time they changed to a little branch line and a train that puffed fussily along the shores of the Moray Firth.

'Fort George.'

They were there. This was the terminus.

Dodd's heart sank as he gazed at the bleak stones of the massive eighteenth century ramparts.

Built after the '45 Rebellion as part of the pacification of the Highlands, it was linked with General Wade's famous military road and had excited the admiration of a certain General Wolfe when he saw it under construction in 1751. King George II had been graciously pleased to permit sixteen acres of bastions and barracks to bear his name. George Dodd, tramping under the classic arch bearing the heraldic device of his royal namesake, was not so enthusiastic. To him it looked like a prison and he was not surprised when someone told him later that night that in 1815 the authorities had thought of keeping Napoleon there instead of at St Helena.

Like a great religion the British regimental system is made up of many mysteries. It encompasses precedence, legend, tradition and (something quite different) custom. It involves memory, personalities, instinct, style and faith. Whatever he may be before he enters it a man subjected to its influences will be changed.

In 1938 Britain was still suffering from the effects of the slump and there were plenty of refugees from the dole queues in Dodd's batch of recruits. There were also one or two miners escaping from the tyranny of the pits. And to his relief there were a number of English lads.

Not that it mattered much where you came from once inside the Depot. It was the Regiment that counted. 'The Regiment' is a generic term covering all who serve in its off-shoots as well as its regular battalions. These had been formed towards the end of the eighteenth century by the Mackenzies of the ancient House of Seaforth in order to give some congenial occupation to their unruly followers now they were forbidden to make war on other Scots. The sponsorship of the lairds, however, did not preclude the recruitment of outsiders and scores of Lowlanders and seventy Englishmen and Irish made the first battalion up to more than 1,000 all told. Dodd was merely one of a long line of Sassenachs to serve in the Seaforths.

No time was wasted in issuing tartan trews to new arrivals at the Depot and they were immediately measured for the kilt. Only after a month had passed were they allowed out in uniform, so long as they could pass the guardroom inspection. This included walking over a mirror to ensure that they were not wearing anything which might be considered unmanly. They had to be ready, too, to answer any question that might be put to them about the Regiment's history as contained in a booklet issued to all recruits – *A Short History of the Seaforth Highlanders.*

A man was expected to know that the Regiment had won ten Victoria Crosses in the Indian Mutiny, of which eight had gone to the 2nd Battalion, then the 78th Highlanders. The Victorian era was made to seem like yesterday. Bearded giants with striking white cap covers hanging over their necks, the 78th featured in dozens of paintings of incidents during the Mutiny when they had won the admiration of the Empire before Lucknow. General Sir James Outram had told them: 'Your exemplary conduct . . . I can truly say and do most emphatically declare, has never been surpassed by any troops of any nation in any age, whether for indomitable valour in the field or steady discipline in camp, under an amount of fighting, hardships and privations such as British troops have seldom been exposed to.'

On the return of the survivors to Fort George in 1859 the 78th were feted at Nairn and Inverness.

The 1st Battalion, the 72nd Highlanders, was equally prominent in the subcontinent during the arduous Afghan War of 1879 and had formed a colourful kilted line at Atbara in the Sudan in 1898 where the followers of the Mahdi were defeated.

With her affection for Scotland, it is little wonder that the Seaforth Highlanders (the 72nd and 78th were linked under the army reforms of 1881) were favourites of Queen Victoria. The 1st Battalion had borne the title of The Duke of Albany's Own Highlanders since 1823 and in later years the Queen made a request that Seaforth officers should wear the cypher and coronet of her son Leopold, Duke of Albany, between the antlers of the stag's head badge.

Though it gave yeoman service during the Boer and Great Wars, the Victorian aura still hung over the regiment in the Twenties and Thirties and lads who had little knowledge of the geography of their own country could accurately describe the streets of Lucknow in Mutiny days.

Along with the fighting record went a great sporting tradition. The other ranks were expected to play soccer and to box. Athletics were also greatly encouraged and prizes ranging from 10s to the magnificent sum of £4 attracted large entries for rifle competitions – a financial inducement that undoubtedly led Private Dodd to become a marksman.

The Seaforths ate well, much better than the average working man. There were four meals a day from Monday to Friday – tea and supper being combined at the weekend when most men got a leave pass. Recruits got tea and biscuits at a mid-morning break and the use of the regimental boat on the Firth sometimes meant that salmon and trout featured on the menu.

At the end of nine weeks' training at the Depot the newcomers were posted to a battalion and, as in Dodd's case, most of them went to the 2nd then located at Maryhill Barracks, Glasgow, the 1st Battalion being in the Far East.

After sleeping only five to a room at Fort George, the crowded conditions at Maryhill did not impress him but this drawback was made up for by increased social opportunities. Glasgow prices were low and a soldier's pay was good. A private might earn between two shillings and 4s 3d a day, depending on his trade and skills. A first-class shot got another 3d a day and a marksman 6d. A soldier who gained a first-class education certificate was also paid extra. With four of his 14s basic pay withheld in credit and a few pence docked for barrack damages, Dodd considered himself well off, especially when he qualified as a driver and got 6d a day trade pay.

With comparative wealth went danger and responsibility. Women haunted the area of the barracks. Any virile Jock who wished to indulge his passions had merely to repair to a cook-shop round the corner, order pie and peas twice, walk out and hold up a dish in each hand. Within minutes he would have a companion and the dubious delights of the canal bank were his. The risks inherent in such liaisons were driven home to newcomers in a salutary fashion. They were detailed for fatigue parties employed in the section of the barracks where soldiers were treated for venereal disease. The screams of the unfortunate patients subjected to some of the drastic and brutal remedies then in vogue had a cautionary effect on the amorous inclinations of all but the most foolhardy. Men went white at the very mention of the word 'umbrella'.

Saturday nights at Maryhill saw sights usual outside barracks, but there was little serious violence. It was also the depot of the Highland Light Infantry but the two regiments got along well, helped, perhaps, by the fact that one battalion of the HLI (Hell's Last Issue) was stationed at Fort George. Within the Seaforths, arguments arose from time to time about religion but the factions kept their quarrels within the battalion. Private Dodd only once saw an unpleasant example of sectarianism. Having gone to the station to pick up some leave men, he had accounted for all except a Private Fox. A search discovered the missing man lying on the platform behind some luggage trolleys. Hair matted with blood, eyes so swollen he could hardly see, Private Fox was still able to mumble through his shattered teeth: 'They've battered Jimmy, but they've no' got his lily.'

Jimmy was a Protestant. Clutched in one hand were the tattered remains of his orange lily, worn on 12 July. It took the medical orderlies who treated his wounds some time to loosen Jimmy's grip on the flower.

Soon afterwards a number of the toughest Seaforths – some with 'Religion: RC.' recorded in their paybooks – slipped out of barracks in search of soldiers from the Scottish Horse.

The yeomanry regiment had to be shown that if any of their ilk picked on a single Seaforth, for whatever reason, be he Protestant, Papist, Presbyterian, Wee Free or Jew, they had to answer to the whole battalion.

The Munich Crisis did not make much impression on the young regular soldiers. There were too many other important matters demanding their attention: guards, drills, parades. The subject of Hitler and the German Army came up from time to time, but hadn't they been told by one of their officers that the Jerry tanks were made of cardboard?

In the spring of 1939, after conscription had been introduced in Britain, there were new faces around – 'militia men', some more willing than others to be soldiers. With summer came the reservists for re-training, bewildered to find that the Lewis gun was a thing of the past, that the last of the horse transport was going and that ten tracked armoured carriers were part and parcel of an infantry battalion.

At the end of August the battalion was in camp at Scampton, Linolnshire. There on 1 September they heard the news that Germany had invaded Poland. That night Lights Out had just been sounded and Private Dodd and the other drivers were chatting in bed when the MT sergeant put his head into the hut and yelled, 'Stand to!' Orders to strike camp followed. They loaded their lorries and drove in convoy all night to Glasgow. At Maryhill they spent much of Saturday unloading and storing equipment. The following morning they were told to listen to the wireless. Sitting on their beds in the barrack room at 11.15 Dodd and his companions heard Mr Chamberlain, the British Prime Minister, announce that a state of war existed with Germany.

The younger, more carefree spirits cheered. Some men looked thoughtful. A few were plainly dejected. Dodd tried to persuade himself that this war would not be as bad as the last, as made out by his father who had been gassed as well as wounded.

The 2nd Seaforths were not in the first four divisions to go to France. They spent their time in exercises around Glasgow with a surfeit of route marching to toughen up the feet of the reservists. Then they moved to Aldershot where they joined the 17th Brigade,* with the 2nd Royal Scots Fusiliers and the 2nd Northamptonshire Regiment, before going on 48 hours' embarkation leave. On their return they heard the incredible news that they would have to give up the kilt.

The kilt, in the Mackenzie tartan, had been worn by the Seaforths since they were formed as the 78th Foot in 1793. The senior battalion, raised fifteen years earlier, had also worn it until 1809. Then, for no good reason as far as anyone could see, by an order approved by George III, they had to give up the kilt and the yellow facings of a Highland regiment and don the uniform of a line battalion, pantaloons, white facings and all.

The 72nd Foot soldiered on in this unwelcome garb for fourteen years, when George IV, as inexplicably as his eccentric father, confirmed an order that they should become a Highland regiment again. There was one condition – they should wear tartan trews instead of the kilt. This they did until the Army reforms of 1881 linked the 72nd and 78th as two battalions of the same regiment. Many were the blessings showered on Queen Victoria when she requested that the senior battalion should also wear the kilt in recognition of its distinguished service in Afghanistan.

'A Highlander in the kilt is a man and a half,' said those who favoured it.

Not everyone agreed with them in 1939. Opponents quoted the view attributed to a French officer that the garment was convenient for *l'amour* but impractical for *la guerre* and particularly *la guerre moderne*.

* Part of the 5th Division, all regular battalions.

In the South African War the Highland Brigade had been pinned down for hours under the blazing sun at Magersfontein and many Jocks suffered severe burns to the backs of their legs. In the mud of Flanders, after the Germans began to use mustard gas in 1917, kilted regiments were said to have suffered more blistering than others through the contact of bare flesh with contaminated ground. In that war, too, the pleats of the kilt had proved to be ideal breeding grounds for lice.

So the kilts were handed in, and shortly thereafter Dodd found himself sailing for France in a brand new battledress ahead of the rest of the battalion.

After a night out in Southampton he returned with some cheerful souls who thought it would be a good idea to let down most of the tents in the transport lines. Not everyone was amused and as a punishment the culprits were given the task of guarding the vehicles in the bowels of the ship taking them to France. To his great surprise Dodd was made responsible for the detachment.

'And heaven help you if there is as much as a scratch on those lorries when you take them off at Cherbourg,' warned the MT officer.

III

Oh, to be in Shanghai

Private Drayton was crawling through the standing corn with his rifle pushed before him in the best fieldcraft handbook manner when a hand fell on his shoulder. Had he been in a position to do so he would have turned and blazed away there and then. Instead his head shot round and he found himself confronted by the unshaven, homely features of a familiar face.

'Doddy! You bastard! What the hell are you doing here?'

'What're you?'

'We're escaping with our officer, Mr Broad.'

'Has the battalion definitely had it, then?'

'Looks like it. Everybody else has cleared off.'

'I'd better come along then.'

While this conversation was taking place the file of escaping soldiers had been drawing away and when Drayton resumed his course the man ahead had vanished. On reaching open ground at the end of the corn he assumed the other Jocks had reached a distant wood and broke into a gallop to catch up. Hoarse shouts made him realize that he was running past a small copse where the party had taken cover. The figures in the wood ahead were Germans, fortunately of the unobservant sort. Drayton rejoined his comrades, gasping. Then Dodd emerged.

The first thought that entered the head of Second-Lieutenant Broad was to put a bullet into the stranger. Hardly a day had passed recently without some alarm about Fifth Columnists. Spies and saboteurs were said to be everywhere. If all the nuns reported to have been seen in

jackboots had been captured they would have filled a convent. As for
bogus staff officers, there must have been a regiment of Nazi tailors
producing uniforms for them. Bearing in mind the calamity which had
occurred, Broad might be excused for deciding to take no chances.
Besides, this dark-chinned brute with shaggy hair looked a potentially
ugly customer. Nor had he been there when they set off. Broad reached
for his revolver. Just why a Fifth Columnist should bother to tack
himself on to a handful of exhausted soldiers when there were more
interesting tasks to perform did not cross his mind. His brain was still
reeling from the events of the day.

'Who do you say you are?'

'Dodd, sir. MT. I was with "D" Company.'

'I don't recognize you. I thought I knew all the drivers.'

Drayton broke in.

'He's OK, sir. That's Dodd all right. We were on the same recruits'
course. He followed me when we went into the field.'

'Anyone else know this man?'

Sergeant Chalmers stepped from the shadows. 'That's Dodd, sir. I
know him.' It was clear from his tone that not everything he knew
about Dodd was commendable.

Broad deliberated in silence. His party, including himself, was
already seven strong. Did they really want an eighth? At the same time
could he possibly turn him away?

'He's not a bad mechanic, sir. So I've heard.' Sergeant Chalmers
had discovered something in Dodd's favour. 'He might be useful if we
find a vehicle.'

'All right, Dodd, it's up to you. You weren't in my platoon and if
you don't want to come with us you don't have to. If you do, well,
you'll do as you're told. Understand?'

'I'll come with you, sir.'

The long crawl through the corn, with German voices and vehicles
clearly audible, had been a strain and Broad was glad of the opportunity to rest in the shade. They had left the battalion's last position so hurriedly that he had had no time to take stock of the men.
He did so now and concluded that they were hardly an impressive
sight. Dirty and dishevelled, one or two were, like himself, wearing
greatcoats; others were in battledress. Each man had his rifle and
equipment, however, and each produced at least one clip of ammunition from his pouches. Broad had his revolver and a few rounds
and was carrying a grenade in a coat pocket. His assets included

field glasses, a partially full whisky flask and a compass. He was disappointed to discover that there were only two waterbottles among them, both nearly empty.

One second-lieutenant, one sergeant and six men . . . from a battalion that had landed in France 780 strong.

The fate of the troops holding St Valery and the covering positions round it had been sealed that morning. Hopes of another 'Dunkirk' had vanished. Churchill, who flew back to Britain from Briare that day, had seen Le Havre blazing 8,000 feet below and pondered on the fate of the Scots trapped under the haze to the north. Then enemy aircraft were reported to be strafing shipping and his Flamingo, which had been obliged to set off without a fighter escort, dived to sea level. The French coast vanished from view. The details of the day's events did not filter through to the Prime Minister until later.

White flags had been seen in St Valery soon after 8 am, though resistance continued in some quarters. The French Corps Commander sent a personal note to General Fortune confirming that he had ordered a ceasefire but Fortune refused to comply until 10.30. By that time he knew for certain that fog had prevented the Royal Navy from reaching the port. Now German guns lined the cliffs.

Twelve generals fell into Rommel's hands that day and he recorded: 'A particular joy for us was the inclusion among them of . . . the commander of the 51st British Division and his staff.'

The reduction of the scattered remnants still holding out presented the Germans with a problem, not least because few of the British units knew what was going on. In the St Sylvain position, held by the battalion headquarters and 'C' Company, the fit survivors of the 2nd Seaforths numbered about a hundred men and there were many wounded. The commanding officer had left some days earlier to take over the 152nd Brigade whose commander had been wounded.

He had been replaced by the second-in-command, a quiet little major with a monocle and a stutter which he disguised by injecting the exclamation 'arragh' into his speech. This officer had never ceased to regret that the outbreak of war had caught him unawares while he was on leave from the 1st Battalion in Shanghai, which he regarded as some sort of paradise. His posting to the 2nd Battalion had filled him with dismay. On assuming command he had done his best, but, as the situation deteriorated, it became clear that he was suffering from concussion and shock and was unable to function efficiently. The next senior major took over, consulting the unfortunate Major from Shanghai only as a formality.

On the night of the 11th hopes had been roused by a Frenchman who offered to guide the troops through enemy lines to the coast. The men fell in and prepared to move. Then the Frenchman learned that it was proposed to take the wounded as well and cried off. The injured would not be able to move fast enough.

They spent the rest of the night formed in a hollow square with the wounded in the middle, a formation Broad found incomprehensible as they were in an open field and offered an easy target. At daylight permission was given for certain individuals to attempt to break out and investigate the situation elsewhere. One of these volunteers, a colour-sergeant, was soon back with the news that he had been captured and taken before a German officer who told him that the battalion would be given until 6 pm to surrender. Heavy artillery was trained on the position and infantry reinforcements would arrive during the day. Failure to capitulate would result in the battalion being 'destroyed'.

The few officers left were called together to discuss this ultimatum. Never in their history had the Seaforths surrendered and some thought it would be a disgrace to do so. Captain Ian Hobkirk, son of a general, went so far as to say that he would never be able to face his family again. He would rather die fighting. The superseded second-in-command, though still dazed and confused, had lost none of his fighting spirit and kept on repeating: 'We must die like gentlemen.'

Broad did not agree. Though only a subaltern, he was nearly thirty and, with a business career in the City behind him, he could draw on experience that extended beyond the Army. As a supplementary reserve officer he was aware that he was sometimes thought of as being a civilian at heart, but he had served in France as long as anyone and had no hesitation in putting forward his own view.

As he saw it, the first duty of the remaining officers was to the men. It might be heroic for them to die fighting but could they really ask the other ranks to sacrifice their lives? Let the wounded, weary and worn out surrender. Those who wished to try to escape – and that included himself – should be free to do so.

The reaction to this was an uneasy silence . . . as if he had suggested something rather unsporting, almost caddish. The atmosphere was broken when their attention was drawn to a detachment of soldiers formed up in three ranks on the road where a car had driven up.

Broad and Hobkirk went over to find out what was going on. They found themselves face to face with a German officer standing beside a big Mercedes in which a driver sat staring stolidly ahead.

'What the hell do you think you're doing?' snapped the two Scots in unison to the sergeant in charge of the detachment.

The German ignored them, climbed back into his car and drove off without a word.

'He told me there's been a ceasefire, sir. Everybody else has surrendered,' said the sergeant. 'It's supposed to be official. I had to get the men fell in.'

'Well you can get them fell out again,' he was told. 'There's been no surrender here.'

It was only on their way back across the field that Broad and Hobkirk realized that they had never thought of shooting the Germans.

By this time Major Murray Grant, the acting CO, had taken a firm decision. The men would be given the choice of either escaping in groups with an officer or of remaining behind with the wounded to surrender. With the exception of the padre, who felt it his duty to stay with the wounded, the officers dispersed to the scattered detachments to explain the situation. Broad, who had been acting as second-in-command of his company, found five men of his platoon waiting for him – the platoon sergeant, his servant, his runner and two riflemen. If there was going to be a break-out they were coming with him. They were Sergeant Chalmers and Privates Turner, Thompson, Osborne, McDonagh and Drayton.

With time running out the would-be escapers gathered round the only serviceable map and tried to pick out a route. One or two decided to head for the coast but Broad and two other young officers chose to head inland, reasoning that unless they could find boats on the beaches they would be trapped. Broad took a compass bearing for a point on the Seine and made some rough notes. Not far from him Major Godfrey Murray waved his cromach and shouted, 'Who's to the beach with me?' He saw his own company commander approach the brave, but still bemused, second-in-command and say, in an anxious voice, 'Well, Andrew, what do you think of things now?'

Without a trace of fear the little man adjusted his monocle and remarked simply, 'I wish, arragh, to God I was in Shanghai.'

The once bustling wood began to empty fast. As on a cricket ground after a big match only strays and debris remained, but here the lingerers were the wounded and the dead, the rubbish empty ammunition boxes, wrecked vehicles and smouldering stores. Broad and his small party crossed the path of a corporal leading another group as they made their way through the wood, then bumped into Hugh Mackenzie, commissioned into the regiment from the London Scottish. The officers shook hands, wished each other goodbye and good luck and parted. Minutes later Broad and his men rushed across a road into the cover of a cornfield, sped on their way by a German tank which unexpectedly rattled round a bend in the road. Its crew failed to see them. Panting from their exertions and shaken by their escape, they rested for a minute.

The 2nd Battalion The Seaforth Highlanders as Broad had known it was no more. The solid structure on which they had all depended had vanished. There was no quartermaster to feed them, no medical officer to tend them, no transport officer to move them, no padre to turn to with their personal problems, no more leave and no more pay. There was not even a superior officer to take the blame if things went wrong. It was all up to him.

Second-Lieutenant Richard Broad at the beginning of the war.

Robert Osborne. Photograph taken in France in 1941.

James McDonagh at the end of the war.

George Dodd in 1938.

Sam Thompson.

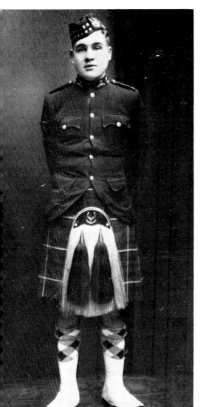

IV

Serious Officers All

Richard Broad's military career began about the same time as Private Dodd's but not in quite the same manner. To begin with his motives were different. He was not seeking a career. He could see war coming and was determined that if he was going to be involved in it he would find a role suited to his station in life. Stockbrokers do not necessarily make good private soldiers any more than most private soldiers are natural stockbrokers.

Like Dodd he had been considered delicate as a boy, having suffered from asthma to an extent that he was unable to attend public school and had to have a private tutor. Perhaps because of this he devoted considerable time to building himself up and became a passable weight-lifter and boxer and played cricket for Tunbridge Wells Eccentrics. In 1938 he stood 6 feet 1 inch tall and tipped the scales at over 14 stone. He was also the deputy senior partner in the firm of W. A. Simpson & Co, brokers to the big tobacco companies, and was married with two children.

For a variety of reasons the idea of joining the Supplementary Reserve of Officers appealed to him. This would enable him to do five weeks' training a year with a regular battalion over a period of two years and then three weeks' training for each subsequent year. This struck him as a far more attractive way of becoming a part-time soldier than doing two drills a week and an annual camp as a Territorial.

His decision to seek entry to a Scottish regiment arose from his family's origins in the Western Isles. Whereas the Seaforths might take

a Sassenach as a soldier they would not have one as an officer. There
was only one vacancy remaining for a Supplementary Reserve Officer
in the regiment and he was aware that others were after it. In the end
he achieved his goal in a very gentlemanly way, making an appointment through proper military channels to be interviewed by the
Colonel of the Regiment, Major-General Sir Archibald Buchanan
Ritchie, at the Army and Navy Club.

The patriarchal system may not appeal in an egalitarian age but it
has its merits. Colonels of Regiments – as opposed to the commanding
officers of battalions – serve as the head of a family. They are invariably
distinguished senior officers who know the customs, traditions and
nature of their regiments intimately. Sir Archibald was just such a
shrewd old warrior, having joined the Seaforths in time to take part in
the Sudan campaign of 1898 and going on to fight in the South African
War and the Great War in which he rose to divisional command.
Broad met him at 11.30, talked of cricket, golf and rugger, and by the
time the General departed to catch a train from Paddington at 12.30
had been told that the vacancy was his. The Army had hardly been
mentioned but Sir Archibald had been convinced that Broad would fit
in.

Once he had passed his medical examination, at which no mention
was made of his asthma, and his application for a commission had been
formally gazetted, Broad was in a position to buy the required items of
uniform. These, similar to those of a regular serving officer, cost £200,
which, even with a government allowance of £40, was a huge sum for
that day, equal to a year's wages for many a working man. The dress of
Highland regiments, cost more than that of the Guards, whereas officers
in some county regiments had been known to kit themselves out on
their government grant.

It did not occur to the adjutant at Fort George that any gentleman
might not play tennis so it was as well for Broad that he did. When he
arrived at the Depot for his first training session he discovered he had
been entered for all events in the annual tournament, held at Nairn a
few miles away, and that partners, male and female, had been found
for him. It was tea and tennis from the moment he arrived. The
serenity of the Moray Firth was undisturbed by the rumblings in
Europe.

The regimental machinery for absorbing new blood then purred
into life and Broad was introduced to his servant, whom he shared
with another officer, and instructed in some of the niceties of Mess

Rules such as the need to wear trews at breakfast and to change into civilian clothes either after lunch or after duty. He learned that no one was addressed by his christian name for the first six months of service life, warrant officers commissioned as quartermasters being the only exception. Lounge suits were worn in the Mess in the evening unless there was a guest night when he must appear in the splendour of his costly mess kit.

Broad had a sergeant to himself as an instructor,* and, though he once managed to be in the wrong place throughout the duration of a church parade, he acquitted himself quite well.

Having also shown himself to be socially acceptable on the tea, tennis and cocktails circuit, he was paid a great compliment – he was considered suitable to complete his training with the 2nd Battalion at Maryhill instead of returning to the depot as was usual. Broad never did finish his formal training as a Supplementary Reserve Officer, though he put in five more weeks in 1939 when the 2nd Battalion, still kilted, went on manoeuvres. A few days before war was declared he took it on himself to drive to Fort George and report for duty. Soon afterwards he was posted to Maryhill.

In the weeks that followed, the battalion almost got back to its peacetime routine. Officers left cards at addresses on the approved social list for Glasgow, and the Commanding Officer, who had ordered all sports kit to be packed ready for a sudden move, decided to unpack it again. The annual competition for the Old Soldier's Trophy would be held after all. Forthwith orders arrived for a move to Aldershot, en route for France.

A bit of a dogsbody is probably the best way in which one could describe Broad's duties at this time. Apart from commanding No. 13 platoon he was battalion messing officer, responsible for the men's food. The latter post brought him into regular contact with the hard-eyed quartermaster, Captain Frank Harris, who had served as a sergeant in the Great War and whose idea of inspiring newly arrived second-lieutenants was to describe how he had seen a subaltern in the Argylls shoot himself during the stress of battle. A better tutor in the ways of the old soldier could not have been found. Broad saw him caught out only once. The ship in which they sailed for France was 'dry' and he and the QM went to some lengths to 'acquire' a crate of Bulmer's cider seemingly abandoned on the quayside. Not only did it turn out to be full of empties but they found it almost impossible to lose

* Sergeant Marle.

and were pursued off the ship by well-meaning people carrying the box they had 'left behind'.

The quartermaster soon made up for this sobering experience in Cherbourg. Sharing a compartment with him on their first train journey, Broad awoke to find his travelling companion tugging at one of his boots, unable to tell which feet were his own.

The Seaforths travelled by Le Mans in Brittany to Seclin on the French border with Belgium. There, after the initial novelty, they settled down to the Phoney War and to building defences. From time to time they moved along the border, but the work remained the same.

It was a testing time for them all, but it gave the officers a chance to learn more about their men.

Many differences which arose had their origins in the rivalry between the two Seaforth regular battalions. Officers from the 1st were considered by some of the other members of the mess to have enjoyed too good a life in the Middle and Far East. Their map-reading and physical fitness were called into question. They were also apt to resent outsiders. The second-in-command was heard to say at dinner one evening that there were 'too many civilians in this war'. This stung one officer of august military lineage, who had left the service after many years and had now been recalled, to leap to his feet and snap, 'Sir?'

To the younger and reserve officers and newcomers like the medical officer, the older hands seemed addicted to protocol and blind obedience; they in their turn appeared to their seniors to ask too many questions and to cut too many corners.

In their different ways both parties sensed that there was something radically wrong with the way the war was going. There was a terrible sense of anticlimax. At the bottom of all their problems was boredom. That was the real enemy – boredom that led the Jocks into estaminets where, for a bet, they would try to drink a glass from every bottle behind the bar.

Lord Gort, Commander-in-Chief of the British Expeditionary Force, was well aware of the problem. He worked in a château near Arras in an office deliberately furnished in spartan fashion. His desk was a scrubbed board table on trestles. A map of the Western Front covered one wall and he stressed to one distinguished visitor* that, though he was responsible for a line stretching from Lille to Douai, he had nothing in front of him except a neutral country.

* André Maurois, the French writer, then serving as a liaison officer.

'In these circumstances it is not easy to keep up the fighting spirit. In the last war the enemy saw to it that the men in the trenches were occupied. Now I'm afraid they will simply be bored.'

Various remedies were tried to break the monotony of interminably digging anti-tank ditches or pouring concrete into pillbox frames. Occasional moves to other locations served only to irritate all ranks. At Halluin, which straddled the Franco-Belgian border, some of the more irreverent officers of the Seaforths had a brainwave.

Broad, accompanied by the battalion interpreter, was engaged in finding billets when he encountered a lady who said she had two good rooms available – but her lodgers would have to be 'serious officers' as she had a daughter. He promptly allocated the rooms to two of the wilder spirits and they formed what they dubbed the 'Serious Officers' Club'.

The club adopted as its headquarters a bistro in the Rue de la Gare, run by a blonde called Betty, who kept open a back door and a back room after closing time. There Eric Finlayson would play the piano just as long as his glass was replenished. Besides him, Broad's fellow-members included McKillop, the Medical Officer, Ian Hobkirk, Eric Finlayson and Roland Mourot.

Roland Mourot was a Lorrainer who had been teaching English at a school a few miles from Nancy when war broke out. Dressed in a uniform which looked far too grand for a mere corporal-interpreter, he approached his appointment to the 2nd Seaforths with some trepidation. His duties would require him to be in constant contact with the Commanding Officer and other officers and he was well aware of the gulf which existed between officers and men in the French Army. The Seaforths solved the problem simply by making him an honorary member of the Officers' Mess. From the beginning he was made to feel at home. When Colonel Iain Barclay told him he would send him a Seaforth kilt when the war was over he felt that he really had been accepted into the family circle.

It seemed to him that all the officers came from the same corner of Scotland and knew not only each other but their families too. When a ham appeared in the mess its origin was quickly identified. Captain So-and-so's mother had sent it. These Scots even knew the secrets of each other's kitchens. The memory of that ham returned to Mourot later on unhappier occasions.

He noted that though officers returned dirty and muddy from trench-digging each evening they reappeared spotless in the mess to have a drink or two before dining 'rather solemnly', the CO presiding.

The behaviour of the other ranks was also a surprise. During the festive season the Jocks zig-zagged their way back to their billets without a single incident to disturb the peace.

To Mourot this was not war as he had expected it. There was no fighting and there were no casualties. Yet he knew the reality of the beast, for he had visited his father's grave at Verdun. By the spring of 1940 Mourot had experienced only one moment of glory. Requested by the medical authorities to check, for reasons of hygiene, on the availability of contraceptives in a local maison de rendezvous he asked the madame if she required any.

'How many have you got on you?' she asked.

'Oh, about four hundred.'

'*Formidable,*' came the reply, 'and you look such a nice boy.'

At Halluin the routine of training and navvying continued in deplorable weather. In the snow and rain the most exciting visitations were epidemics of German measles and influenza. These gave meaning to the life of the medical officer who had become neurotic about squatting in an ambulance dealing with mythical casualties suffered on manoeuvres. Recently qualified, the doctor had held a low opinion of the Services ever since he had been unable to obtain enough serum to give anti-tetanus injections to the whole battalion. In one quest for supplies he had worked his way steadily upwards through the hierarchy of a military hospital telling them they did not know their jobs until the final victim of his wrath revealed himself to be the Director of Medical Services himself. The MO returned somewhat scorched from the encounter but with the serum.

This humdrum existence was relieved to some extent by the news that the battalion was to join the 51st Highland Division. A Territorial Army formation with a fine record in the Great War, it had come to France in 1940 full of enthusiasm but short of experience.

To redress the balance regular battalions were exchanged and the 2nd Seaforths switched with the 6th in the 152nd Brigade. To many of the Jocks the move was welcome. The 51st Division was highly rated in the propaganda stakes and frequently appeared in newspapers and on newsreels. Many had relatives in the ranks. Not everyone was so enthusiastic and the Commanding Officer of the 2nd Battalion regarded it almost as a slight to be transferred to what was to all intents a raw formation. Relocation in the Bailleul area, where the 51st had been cut to pieces in the German Flanders offensive in April, 1918, did not provide a good omen. Kilted corpses were still being unearthed. The order to move to the supporting defences of the Maginot Line, which were actually in contact with the enemy, came as a great relief to all. In a bout of nostalgia the Serious Officers' Club travelled to Halluin for one last party in which the Medical Officer survived a fall down a flight of fourteen stairs without serious injury. The next morning the battalion entrained for the Saar and the transport set off by road.

Private Dodd learned for the first time on the Saar that casualty lists did actually include one's pals. On the evening the battalion transport arrived in the sector the lorries were directed to a wooded valley. 'Big' McFarlane swung his vehicle wide before driving under the trees. A brilliant flash was followed by a swirl of smoke and a crash which echoed round the gloomy slopes. Pieces of metal were still falling when Dodd heard the distant report of the gun that had fired the solitary shell. He had witnessed the battalion's first fatal battle casualty.

The 2nd Seaforths did not have a happy time on the Saar. They occupied posts on the Line of Contact some fifteen miles in advance of the Maginot Line where the previous French occupants had subscribed to that debatable military theory that it is sometimes better to live and let live than to stir things up. All initiative seemed to have passed to the enemy and the defences themselves were unimpressive. The theory proved to be highly contagious and Broad found himself being soundly berated by one of his superiors for wishing to bring machine-gun fire down on a group of Germans he had spotted working within easy range.

Aggressive night patrolling by the enemy subjected the Highlanders to constant strain. Exhaustion through lack of sleep became a problem; but they began to learn. Lights which appeared beyond the apron wire at night were not fired on. They were almost certainly the work of Germans safely under cover trying to get their opponents to give away their positions. Grenades – if the target was thought to be near enough – were the order of the day. Once Broad was horrified to see a small light *inside* the wire defences and crept forward, revolver in hand, to within point blank range of a glow-worm.

The opening of the Blitzkrieg was announced by the passage over the lines of droves of enemy planes on the night of 9 May, but the first heavy attacks on the 51st did not come until three days later. These

were beaten off, but not without casualties. An outpost reported the
Germans massing for another attack and an artillery observer came
up, but he could see nothing. The weary Jocks were beginning to
imagine things.

Withdrawal to the Line of Recoil between the forward posts and the
Maginot Forts did nothing to lighten the strain. There was little wire,
no sandbags, no shelter for the men and no stores. Broad took a lorry
and helped himself from an unguarded British dump. It was as well he
did because the Recoil Line soon became the front line and the nerve-
wracking business of patrolling and being probed by enemy patrols
began all over again. He set out one night with five men to explore an
abandoned dugout but missed it in the dark and took up a position
nearby. Footsteps were heard coming and going and the following day
marks in the damp earth showed that the Germans had passed unseen
within thirty feet of him.

It became fashionable at this time to slate the French for all short-
comings. The phrase 'France would fight to the last Englishman' was
as common in British circles as its counterpart 'England would fight to
the last Frenchman' was current in French.

The Seaforths left the Maginot Line area after a difference of opinion
between the CO and the commander of the incoming French unit
about the times of relief. They were not sorry to go.

V

Jimmy Stepforit . . .

It was his total ignorance of what was going on elsewhere that frustrated Second Lieutenant Broad as he lay in hiding waiting for dusk. News had been scarce since leaving the Saar. They had learned of the rest of the BEF's departure from Dunkirk only after it had gone. He was uncertain if the French Army was still resisting, though the previous day twenty *chasseurs à pied* had fought alongside the Seaforths until their captain had been killed. Then they had drifted away, correctly anticipating events.

It occurred to him that Le Havre might be in allied hands for the moment but it was a dead end between the Channel and the Seine estuary and unless they could find a boat they would be trapped. Rouen was almost certainly in enemy hands but the Seine wound snake-like from the ancient Norman capital to the sea and the Germans could not possibly police the entire length. In any case, they probably had no need to. His idea of taking a compass bearing for Duclair, a town to the west of Rouen, a distance of about forty miles, seemed to offer the best hope. If they could find inconspicuous transport they would use it, otherwise they would march. Their first objective must be to get out of the immediate area of St Valery.

Escape and evasion exercises not then being part of army training, Broad improvised his own rules. He would move by night and lie up during the day. After dark the Jocks formed single file and set out, the sergeant bringing up the rear.

When it began to grow light the party went to ground at the edge of another wood and slept for a while.

They awoke two or three hours later to the sound of revving engines and men's voices. They had bivouacked alongside an enemy unit. Creeping away one by one, they spent the rest of the day hidden in the long grass of an uncut meadow. German transport horses watched them for some time, then lost interest. Later their drivers arrived to attend to them and one or two passed within feet of the hiding place. Only a Frenchman, whom Broad guessed was the owner of the field, noticed their presence. As he passed with a woman, probably his wife, he warned her to be careful not to tread on '*les Anglais*'.

As the day drew on Broad began to wonder, in view of the concentration of German troops in the area, whether he had done the right thing to head inland, into their midst, instead of trying to escape to the beaches.

Roland Mourot had been almost too weary to crawl away from the shambles of the last stand. He was worn out physically and mentally, but still full of admiration for the Highlanders. Sitting on a wall in the battalion headquarters area at St Sylvain the previous day he had noted how stoically the wounded Jocks bore their pain. Very rarely did one of them moan or cry out. On the whole they gritted their teeth in silence.

When the remnants of the battalion formed the improbable hollow square, Mourot watched the reaction of the surviving wounded lying on makeshift stretchers of doors and shutters. They remained phlegmatic and uncomplaining. After the decision to try to escape was taken and it became clear that they would have to be left behind there was not a single sign of panic. Mourot simply tacked himself on to a group of officers and men making for the coast. Despite the ring of tanks round the battalion, they reached the beach, two or three kilometres away, without being seen. There, with a number of officers and men, he took refuge in a cave, the weary Jocks building a barrier of rocks across the entrance. One gallant soul had even swum out to sea to try to contact any small boats thought to be off the shore. On his return he reported that there were still plenty of craft in the area. One was almost sure to attempt to pick them up. Mourot fell into a deep sleep.

'*Raus! Raus!*'

It was dawn and the German shouts were clearly meant for the occupants of the cave. The soldiers lying at their rifles along the primitive barricade looked round questioningly. Mourot stared blearily at the drawn faces of the officers. This time there was nothing for it. The game was up. Machine-guns or grenades would wreak havoc in the enclosed space.

They gave themselves up slowly, blinking in the growing light and were marched to the cliff tops. From there they watched a small warship approach the beach they had just left. An anti-tank gun opened fire and, after a few shots, the vessel turned away without shooting back. They had missed rescue by about an hour. Later that day Mourot was separated from the Seaforths and added to a batch of French prisoners. His captors, baffled by his Ruritanian uniform, accepted his claim to be an officer.

For Broad's party darkness brought only temporary relief. After they had been marching for about an hour they were challenged by a German who opened fire with an automatic weapon as they crossed a field. A herd of cows promptly stampeded around them. With bullets whistling overhead, the Jocks dived beneath a barbed-wire fence and made off. No attempt was made to pursue them, and the Germans lost interest. It became obvious that they belonged to a searchlight detachment when a beam pierced the sky and began searching for a low-flying plane. Other lights joined in and soon the whole landscape was bathed in a harsh glare. The Seaforths froze.

The plane, when it was picked up, flashed signals which must have identified it as a friend since it was not fired on. From the noise of its engines it was clearly in trouble but the searchlight crews did not seem concerned and switched off. The Seaforths, plunged back into darkness, were waiting for their eyes to readjust when the plane developed a deafening throaty roar which seemed to be coming straight at them. As one man they threw themselves to the ground and felt it heave beneath them. A hot blast flattened the grass and brilliant flames leapt skywards only a hundred yards away. The Seaforths fled before anyone arrived to investigate.

Sergeant Chalmers was a lucky man and he knew it. By rights he should have lost his stripes, and possibly worse, weeks earlier while they were on the Saar. Fond of a drink, he had been helped to celebrate his birthday by a number of French NCO's and his platoon commander had considered charging him with being drunk on duty in the face of the enemy. Only a freak accident had saved him. Broad's platoon sergeant had fired into the darkness after challenging three times in the direction of a suspicious noise. His bullet had killed a Seaforth who had improvised a private latrine in the wood they were holding. Though guiltless of any negligence, the sergeant's continued presence in the platoon had become intolerable and an exchange had been agreed. Broad took Chalmers in No. 13 platoon and his friend Hobkirk took on the sergeant who had fired the tragic shot.

The exchange had worked well, though Chalmers had been lucky to get away with another lapse. He had been 'under the influence' again when a sudden order to move arrived. Told to fall in the men, who were aware of his condition, he had shouted, 'Stepforit', sending the platoon gleefully plunging over the edge of the sunken road they were lining.

Occupied with other urgent matters, Broad was unable to deal with the incident there and then and Chalmers managed to avoid him until he was in possession of himself. Henceforth he was known behind his back as 'Jimmy Stepforit'.

Chalmers was the oldest of the escapers. He had 'done his time' with the regiment before the war and had been working for the GPO in Edinburgh when recalled. He regarded membership of a regular Seaforth battalion Sergeants' Mess as the greatest honour that could fall to a man. Of medium height, with greying fair hair, he was tough and lean and had gained a reputation as a Battalion boxer in his younger days.

From the chalk cliffs of the Alabaster Coast that runs from Le Havre to the Somme a monotonous plain stretches inland – the Caux plateau. The isolated half-timbered farms are traditionally shielded from the winds by six-foot-high banks planted with beech and oak. Here the products are dairy as well as arable. In June, 1940, the corn, bright with poppies, was ripening fast in glorious weather but the ears were as yet inedible. The Seaforths found themselves starving in a land that promised plenty. They were also out of water.

The day after the air crash, the party used a wheatfield as a hiding place, intending to wait until nightfall. Hunger, however, got the better of them and Broad and Turner, his redheaded batman, set out to find food.

They were approaching a farmhouse when a large open tourer roared down the drive. Broad got a glimpse of peaked caps as he and Turner dived into the only cover, a field of spring greens. They lay with faces pressed to the earth which had obviously been manured quite recently. A dust cloud swirled over them and the car skidded to a halt

perhaps 75 yards away, Broad guessed. A door slammed as someone
shut it behind them. Had they been spotted? Broad inched his hand to
his holster, acutely aware of the back of his neck. If he heard footsteps
he would wait until he judged the range was right and then . . .

A firm voice rang out in German, bringing a hesitant reply. A curt
sentence silenced what sounded like a mild protest. There was an
obedient 'Jawohl, Herr Hauptmann!' A slammed door again, an urgent
revving and the car was off. A victorious army wasn't going to waste
time chasing shadows. Stuffing spring greens into their battledress
blouses the Scots sneaked back to their comrades.

The unwashed cabbage plants, full of grit, were not a success and
made those who ate them even more thirsty. The Scots lay parched as
German vehicles bustled over the roads criss-crossing the plain. It was
14 June – the day the Germans entered Paris.

The march that evening was exhausting. Broad found himself suffering from palpitations and some of the others were showing signs of
distress. Two tethered cows raised their hopes but all attempts to milk
them failed. The party marched on for some distance before realizing
that Dodd was missing. They returned to the uncooperative cows
where they found the absentee sound asleep under a tree. He was
prodded into life.

A railway line was the saving of them. They followed it to a crossing
where the red and white poles stood raised, the keeper gone, his cottage
empty. In the garden was a well.

In the best Westerns men who find water after days in the desert are
warned on pain of death to drink sparingly. The Seaforths took none of
these precautions but filled themselves almost to bursting point with
the brackish liquid. There were no ill effects.

Broad and Turner had more luck in their foraging the following
day, discovering a jar of salted butter in a deserted house and stumbling across a field of potatoes which were just about large enough
to eat. The small tubers, helped down by the butter, were consumed
raw and pronounced excellent. Twenty-four hours later, with another night's march behind the party, Broad made his first approach
to a civilian since leaving the battalion position. From the shelter of
a wood he saw a woman milking a cow. Covered by Turner, who
always accompanied him on his morning patrol, Broad clambered
down a bank, watched by two small boys. Standing in the middle of
the road he began negotiations over a hedge, the woman still deftly
milking. Discussions were concluded without much difficulty and the

woman promised to send milk and eggs to the copse in which the
men were hidden.

Hardly had Broad said '*Merci, madame!*' when a car was heard and
he had to scramble hurriedly up the bank to rejoin Turner. He drew
his revolver and they waited.

A car containing four men appeared round a bend and braked
opposite. The two small boys now watched impassively as a German
officer entered into conversation with their mother over the hedge.
She, without changing her expression, gave the directions required,
acknowledged another '*Merci, madame*' and watched the car drive off.

The Jocks dined that night on hard-boiled eggs and milk for which
the woman would accept no payment. The food was badly needed, for
they required all their energy the next day to battle their way through
the head-high bracken and brambles of an extensive forest. As they
forced their way through the undergrowth, the Third Republic was
crumbling.

In Bordeaux the French Government was considering the unwelcome
contents of a message from President Roosevelt. Though personally
sympathetic, he said there could be no question of American armed
intervention in the conflict. Weygand's despair was becoming more
pronounced with every situation report. A hysterical outburst later in
the day led President Lebrun to reproach him for his 'intemperate
language'. The next evening Reynaud resigned as Prime Minister and
Lebrun asked Pétain to form a government. The old Marshal produced
a piece of paper with a list of names forthwith. On Monday, 17 June,
Pétain asked for an armistice and General de Gaulle flew to England.
On that day also Richard Broad met the Mayor of Pavilly.

The problem of finding food and shelter eased as the Seaforths
entered a more populous area. They acquired an abandoned primus
stove and some paraffin. A Czech farmer, who had settled in France,
took fifty francs from Broad and bought supplies for them when he
took requisitioned milk to the German garrison in Yvetot. He also
produced wine and spirits which he drank himself after Broad decided
it might be too much of a shock to the men's systems. In appreciation
of the help they had received Broad gave one of the farmer's children
his treasured whisky flask (and contents) and the boy thereupon
brought half a dozen female relatives to view the visitors. The soldiers
left the farm that night to the drunken cheers of the farmer and the
good wishes of his womenfolk. They were considerably heartened when

just before dawn they came across a sign which read 'Pavilly'. Once there they would be in striking distance of the Seine.

For Private Thompson things did not go smoothly at Pavilly. He did not really grasp what was going on. Like many soldiers who have been in close combat he suffered from deafness and occasionally pretended he understood when he didn't. That morning Broad had disappeared with Turner as usual and returned alone to the wood where they were resting. One by one his comrades had crept away. Then it was Thompson's turn. Broad was sending the men across the main road to a hole he had cut in a hedge. Thompson, however, thought they were merely crawling down the road to keep out of sight. Having started, he kept going, rifle and all, straight past the gap. When Broad looked to see if the coast was clear for the next man he was startled to see Thompson disappearing in the distance. It was useless to shout. He had to race after him and drag him back.

Broad had decided to lie up in a shed in the grounds of a bolted and barred château. A helpful old First World War veteran living opposite had promised to bring them food and, while they were waiting for him, the château caretaker arrived. The man seemed friendly and Broad, desperate for news, asked if there was still a mayor at Pavilly. The caretaker set off to fetch him.

After half an hour the shed door opened and in came the mayor, accompanied by the caretaker and his wife. Waiting only to establish which of the fugitives was the officer, he promptly asked Broad to tell his soldiers to hand over their weapons. A wiser man might have looked more closely into the weatherbeaten faces of the men carrying the Lee-Enfields.

'Why?'

'So that I can arrange for you to become prisoners.'

After Broad had explained that they had no intention of surrendering he learned for the first time that the Germans had overrun all the country north of the Seine and were now ninety miles south of it.

Attempts to escape were absurd, said the mayor. If they would hand over their rifles he would arrange matters with the German *kommandantur*.

Broad said that he would have to talk it over with his men. If the mayor promised not to take any action until 2 pm, he would give his answer then. The mayor left.

Broad's first step was to seek out the old soldier he had met earlier. The veteran proved to be highly amused and Broad understood him to say that the mayor was a new man installed by the Germans. He wasn't sure but he might even be of German origin, perhaps an Alsatian.

The Seaforths returned through the hole in the hedge to the wood from whence they had come. This time Thompson kept up.

That afternoon they held a council of war. The position was now far more complicated than it had been and the odds against them were increasing. Some might even feel they had endured enough, said Broad. Each in turn was asked his opinion. All were for going on. The only qualification came from Drayton, who had taken a strong dislike to the mayor and wanted to 'shoot the bugger first'.

VI

One More River

The first attempt to cross the Seine was made on the night of 18 June. It was the 135th anniversary of the battle of Waterloo, but as it had not been one of 'their' battles the Seaforths were unaware of it. Unlike the British relief at Blucher's appearance on that occasion, the arrival of any Prussians would have been most unwelcome.

The non-appearance of the enemy was something of a mystery to the party as it made its way noisily through the streets of the small town of Duclair. There were gasps, curses, stumbles and exclamations. The target of the oaths was a rectangle of wood masquerading as a raft. Its designer, a local *garagiste*, accompanied it to the river with the pride of a naval architect keen to see his latest creation leave the slipway. The four soldiers who bore it on their shoulders were not so enamoured of it.

The raft was the end-product of a busy day which had started with the troops going into hiding in the woods as usual while Broad and Turner searched for provisions. They were gone so long that Chalmers, who had been left in charge, began to think they had fallen into enemy hands. Then, in the distance, he saw a small procession wending its way across the fields. At its head was Broad with a civilian. In the middle were several women with a number of chattering children. At the rear was Turner who kept on stepping over things that weren't there. Chalmers' experienced eye told him the young soldier was trying to conceal a mild state of intoxication. The explanation was simple. The civilians were the occupants of a cottage at which Broad had risked calling. A young couple made him most welcome, insisted he

call Turner from the bushes where he was hiding, and provided them
with an omelette on the spot.

After some discussion the children were despatched to buy bread
and milk with money supplied by Broad. In the meantime the couple
and the children's grandmother plied the two soldiers with drink. This
was too much for Turner. He was slurring his speech when the children
returned with their purchases, but set off with dignified step as he
followed Broad to rejoin the others, accompanied by the whole family,
who saw the expedition as some sort of picnic.

While the men ate, Broad was able to get a firm idea of their location.
They were about three miles from their riverside objective. The bad
news was that there were no boats available. The young Frenchman
was sure of it. However, he had a friend who ran a garage in Duclair,
who was always full of ideas. He would consult him and report back
that night, when his wife would also supply a cooked chicken.

The *garagiste* was one of nature's enthusiasts. When he arrived that
evening, along with the entire complement of original visitors, grandma
and children included, he sang the praises of rafts so sweetly that Broad
was persuaded to try. He was aware that there were rafts and rafts and
that the best were supported by barrels or buoyancy tanks. Even these,
however, showed a marked reluctance to move in the direction
required. Nevertheless the Seaforths, having performed the minor
miracle of dividing a cooked chicken among eight, and having
consumed twenty litres of milk, took their farewells of the peasant
family and accompanied their new-found friend to a local woodyard.
From there they trooped into the night bearing a selection of stout
planks.

At what was declared to be a quiet spot the construction of the raft
began. The *garagiste* had come well provided with heavy hammers and
large nails and these he drove home with complete abandon. The noise
echoed and re-echoed through the night. Duclair, with its enemy
garrison, was only a kilometre distant. When Broad protested the
garagiste expressed contempt for the Germans in strong terms and said
that they got drunk every night and stayed indoors after 8.30, observing
their own curfew.

The completed raft proved to be very heavy, but with some difficulty
it was hoisted on to the shoulders of four men and the party set off
down a railway track. The journey took longer than had been anti-
cipated and from time to time the carriers had to be relieved. Each time
rifles had to be redistributed. Half the party staggered, sweating and

grunting, under the weight of the clumsy contraption, while the rest, encumbered with the weapons of their comrades, plodded alongside. Blindly they followed Broad, who, in his turn, was guided by the *garagiste* who put his trust entirely in the sharp eyes of his young brother, employed to scout the way ahead. When the lad came racing back to report a train standing on the line the party bolted off the track so quickly that the raft fell to the ground. They dragged it into a field of standing corn and lay there. There weren't supposed to be any trains ... and no one had heard a locomotive. Minutes passed in silence before Broad went to look for himself. In the distance, through the gloom, he could make out pale outlines and a dull red light. He crept closer until he identified two deserted Red Cross wagons which had been shunted on to a siding. From ground level he could look up through the windows at jagged holes in the roofs. The train had been machine-gunned from the air and smelled of corpses. Little wonder the guard hadn't remembered to put out the tail light. A nasty business ... but his concern was with the living. They had to get on.

'All right, pick it up lads.'

Pavilly was reached without further incident. Eventually, they came to a level crossing and a wide street where the ammunition boots of the soldiers grated on the cobbles. Still not a curtain twitched, not a door opened.

Finally the raft was deposited on the banks of the river, which appeared to be as wide as the Thames at Tower Bridge.

At this late stage Broad discovered that three of his party could not swim and that his servant, Turner, was only a poor performer. It was decided to leave him and the other non-swimmers, Privates McDonagh, Osborne and Thompson, on the bank with the weapons while Chalmers, Dodd, Drayton and Broad crossed with their clothes and belongings aboard. If all went well they would return for the others. A trial swim showed that there was only a mild current towards the middle of the river and without further ado the four swimmers stripped, piled their clothes on to the clumsy wooden structure and dragged it into the water.

The timber had lain in the yard throughout the summer and was bone dry. As the Seine received the raft the planks absorbed the water greedily. Towards midstream the current's gentle nudging caused the framework to twist and one side began to sink, so Sergeant Chalmers swam round to prop it up. When the opposite side began to sag the others gave a hand, but, after briefly seeming to stabilize itself, the raft was clearly going under.

Having slept through the hammering of the raft's construction and the clamour of the launching ceremony the Germans now slumbered on oblivious to the hoarse shouts of the sergeant who seemed to have been born to save sinking rafts. He darted to and fro, splashing here, pushing there, directing the others where to make their effort. The raft remained churlishly indifferent and sank lower until it was awash. By the time they reached the bank again some of the cargo had gone for ever.

In silence three of them replaced their sodden clothes. Dodd remained naked. His uniform had sunk, along with his size 11 boots.

While the younger Frenchman went to obtain something to cover the shivering Dodd the rest glumly assessed the cost of the venture. Apart from Dodd's clothes, a number of other articles had gone, the most important of which were Drayton's ammunition pouches containing a supply of hard-boiled eggs.

The Frenchman, unabashed by the failure, studied the Jocks curiously when his brother returned with an old coat and ancient trousers, some towels but no shoes. Dodd dressed, muttering as he did so; then his comrades helped him to tie the towels round his feet. Finally Dodd rose and slung his rifle, and they all stepped back to appraise their handiwork. An armed scarecrow confronted them. They looked at each other, tattered, woebegone and three of them sopping wet, and then back at the scarecrow. It was too much. One of them tried to choke back a guffaw but failed. Someone gasped, 'I don't believe it!' and collapsed into laughter.

'It's all right for you lot,' said the lugubrious scarecrow. 'You haven't lost your kit.'

At this all attempts to keep a straight face vanished. The Jocks fell against each other helplessly and the *garagiste*, appreciating the situation though not understanding a word, uttered a succession of high-pitched cackles.

They followed the Frenchman up the railway line towards a barn where he said they could hide. It was full of hay and they spread the wet clothes out to dry before going to sleep. The Frenchman promised to return the next day.

Miles to the south, river crossings were going on that day which were bereft of all sign of humour. The flood of refugees which surged uncontrolled from the north as the Germans advanced had reached the Loire and its narrow bridges. To the enemy planes the bridges were simply military targets and they bombed and machine-gunned them at will in their efforts to prevent demolition by French sappers. At Nantes, in Brittany, where numerous bridges cross the river and canals, a panic developed at a rumour that all were to be blown. A terrified, fighting mob clambered over and around the jam of lorries, cars and carts.

Boats, it seemed, did exist at Duclair. Having waited all day for the return of the *garagiste*, Broad set out to seek help elsewhere. He persuaded a young woman to leave her cottage and buy bread for him, while he and Turner played with her children until she returned. She then introduced them to her father who said he would try to find a boat. Back at the barn Broad had a brief encounter with the farmer's wife, who opened the door and was startled to find she had eight lodgers. Though she made a hasty exit, Broad managed to tell her about their need for transport across the river.

Within hours they had two offers of boats – one arranged by the owner of the barn, whose wife had been paying more attention than she indicated, and one from the father of the young woman who had bought the bread. The first belonged to the local schoolmaster and, to Broad's embarrassment, both he and the young woman arrived about the same time to discuss the matter. Both insisted that the men should cross in *their* boat and the conversation became so heated that Broad retreated to the safety of the barn, fearing lest the dispute would result in no boat at all. He need not have feared. At dusk there was a cautious tap at the barn door and a man appeared and said he would come for them at midnight. Shortly after he had departed a youth arrived and told them to follow him at once. Applying the bird in the hand principle, Broad and his men left immediately and found the schoolmaster waiting outside in the shadows. He scouted ahead and waved them forward when the coast was clear.

The youth rowed them across, then led them through a village on the other side and put them on the road to the town of Montfort where, he understood, they would find British troops. Every franc being precious, Broad rewarded the lad with a ten shilling note. It was well received.

On the second day after crossing the river the Seaforths reached a small town near the edge of the Neubourg Plain, a richer version of the Caux plateau. They had approached across the fields and Broad concealed the party in a shrub-covered lane leading into the town. He then crept into an orchard full of cars and carts and refugees. From these he learned that the British were no longer at Montfort.

Ever the optimist, Broad again sought help from the civic authorities in the shape of the solitary councillor left in the town. This individual proved co-operative in the morning but in the afternoon, having phoned someone further up the municipal hierarchy, he completely reversed his attitude and wanted only to be rid of his unwelcome visitors. They were, he said, bringing danger to the whole community and would they leave as quickly as possible. Couldn't he do anything? Broad asked. Perhaps even hire a train? The councillor merely suggested they head for Honfleur, twenty-five miles away, and produced a map showing them the route. To Broad's dismay this led through a large forest. And to his annoyance the councillor refused him the map, declared it impossible to help with transport and denied them the use of a guide.

Cold with rage, Broad formed his men in file and marched them through the main street. The councillor trotted behind for a while, spluttering with fear and wringing his hands with anxiety. The Seaforths showed only contempt for him.

Broad was proud of his men that day. Throughout their trek he had insisted that they obey certain rules. One was not to steal anything of value or do any unnecessary damage when entering empty houses, as this could annoy the local populace. They might, on this day, have commandeered transport at rifle point, helped themselves to the contents of food shops and bullied the councillor into giving aid. They might even have scoured the town for a pair of boots for Dodd, who had to content himself with ancient relics supplied by the refugees and eased into shape by cutting slits in the uppers.

Instead, under considerable provocation, they behaved in a disciplined, civilized manner. Ragged and ill-shod they may have been, but soldiers they remained.

Broad's plan was to reach Honfleur by a forced march over two days, the first necessity being to pass through the forest which, he hoped, would give them some relief from the heat. Just reaching the place proved exhausting, however, and though he had obtained a Michelin map from some peasants on the way, they were soon lost.

The Brotonne Forest stands on the site of what was a flourishing district of Gallo-Roman villages which were destroyed by barbarians in the Dark Ages. Indiscriminate felling had reduced its once magnificent beech groves to a sorry state by the middle of the nineteenth century when a comprehensive improvement plan was implemented. Thus it was that Scots pines were among the trees that shaded the weary Seaforths.

Broad resorted finally to a compass bearing and, as darkness fell, they marched on in silence, unaware of the ruined civilization under their aching feet, fugitives from a latter-day barbarism.

The leaden legs moved automatically, the throats grew drier and the minds wandered. All bar Dodd had done a march like this on the retreat from the Somme. German artillery had opened up a tremendous bombardment as 'C' company was withdrawing from a village. Dozens of houses had come crashing down and the place burst into flames. The glare had lighted their way for hours. Fifteen miles they had covered after a day of battle, tramping along roads jammed with retreating transport and refugees, over a bridge which was blown two minutes after they crossed. McDonagh and Osborne, both from Paisley, had marched together on that occasion. They remembered how Mr Broad had moved up and down the column like a madman, cursing them, pleading with them, mocking them, to keep them going. They'd had to stop every fifteen minutes towards the end or they would never have made it. Now, in this dark, unlit forest they went on and on, once more practically asleep on their feet.

Dodd's voice interrupted their thoughts. Quietly and without any sign of emotion.

'I'm sorry, sir, but I just cannot walk any further.'

The little column halted.

Dodd's ancient boots had come adrift and the soles were flapping as he walked. He had borne the discomfort and pain for hours without complaint. They did not even bother to find a barn that night but simply slept under the trees.

There are times when soldiers may sleep but their leaders may not. Throughout the night the French General Charles Huntziger, who had seen his troops shattered at Sedan a month earlier, had been making a frustrating journey over crowded roads. His car was one of a line of ten heading against the general flow of traffic to the Loire near Tours. Near Amboise the convoy was flagged down and German motor-cyclists took over escort duties. White flags fluttered from the vehicles speeding down the tree-lined Paris road.

Huntziger's party finally arrived at the Forest of Rethonde where a railway coach stood in a sunlit clearing. Inside was Adolf Hitler. He and his entourage had arrived in a fleet of cars fifteen minutes earlier. In the same setting in which the German armistice delegates had heard their country's fate in 1918 General Keitel began to dictate the Nazi leader's terms.

VII

Ghost Patrol

Broad's private war with French bureaucracy took up much of the next two days. Having led his men out of the Brotonne forest and established a base in the barn of a friendly old farmer, a cripple from the previous war, he entered into negotiations with the mayors of Ste Croix and Aizier, villages equidistant from the hiding place. Neither were of any use. Both refused to supply transport and one said that as far as he was concerned he was now under German orders and that he would see to it that no one else supplied them with so much as a bicycle. This time it was Broad who felt like shooting the collaborator.

Even at this early stage of the war differences were beginning to emerge among the populace and the deputy mayor of Ste Croix quietly put Broad in touch with a man who said he would give them a lift if they could find the petrol. This Broad, despite all efforts, was unable to do and suggested in desperation that he would be grateful for a lift in the man's horse-drawn cart if all else failed. The horse, however, had been working all day and was not up to overtime. Finally the man offered to give them a lift seven of the fifteen miles they were trying to cover. This way he would have enough petrol to return home.

This Samaritan had flair; not only did he produce an old four-seater Citroen but he conjured up enough civilian caps for the men to wear in transit. Somehow they crammed themselves into the vehicle at 9 pm that night and somehow it reached its destination outside the village of Bougleron. Apart from the river crossing, it was the first time in twelve days that they had moved any other way than on their feet. On a beautiful summer's evening they resumed their march to the coast, amusing themselves by describing the sort of meal they would have when they reached England. As a director of the company which owned the South Western Hotel at Southampton, Broad promised to foot the bill – for where else would they land? They would, he said, order the food without changing from their present rags and see how the head waiter received them.

A glimpse of the sea spurred them on as they descended through woods on to the coast road. Then harsh reality returned.

By the side of the road, neatly parked but without any sign of its owner, stood a civilian motor-cycle, its petrol tank full and its panniers stuffed with tins of pilchards. The food was appropriated immediately but Broad wrestled with his conscience about helping himself to a bike belonging to someone else. It could, in any case, be more trouble than it was worth. Someone might start a search for it. Before he could make a decision a vehicle was heard and the Seaforths leaped over the nearest hedge. There wasn't time to look first and they went slithering down a steep slope, their belongings tumbling alongside them. At the bottom they lay still as the engine roared nearer and stopped. The sound of men landing heavily, as if jumping fully armed from a truck, came to them. After an ominous pause a line of heads appeared above the hedge. Crouched in the shadows the Jocks waited. Then it dawned on them. The Germans were relieving themselves. They were laughing and seemed to be enjoying the fading view over the estuary. The Seaforths exchanged glances. The relief was mutual.

There was more shouting before the lorry departed and the roar of a motor-cycle engine told Broad that his dilemma had been resolved for him. He waited a while before leading the men back to the road.

Two houses ablaze with lights next attracted their attention, but a voice called out '*Vass?*' as Broad was about to knock on the door of one of them and he retreated hastily to a ditch where the others were waiting. There was no alternative but to keep going.

The sentry was enjoying his 'stag'. Propped in the gateway of a villa keeping an eye on the vehicle sheds on the other side of the road, he breathed in the balmy night air and counted himself lucky. Perhaps he was contemplating leaving when the first of the 'things' appeared. Round a bend in the road came a shadowy figure wearing a long garment and a strange hat. Behind it came another – and another. The first passed within two feet of his astonished eyes, moving at an even unbroken pace, without glancing to the right or left. Those following seemed to be carrying rifles, but they took no more notice of him than the first. His grip on his own weapon tightened as he counted them: 'Five . . . six . . . seven.'

'*Bonsoimuzoo!*'

The eighth and last of them had uttered a strange cry, making the sentry jump. Swallowing and shaking, he pulled himself together and began to creep gently down the road after them. The grey figures simply drew further and further away until they vanished in the darkness.

What manner of 'things' were they? The sentry thought discretion the better part of valour and returned to his post.

The sentry had taken Broad by surprise and there was no way he could avoid him without causing an alarm. For a second he thought he might be a French soldier, but the silhouetted helmet destroyed that notion. So Broad kept on walking, confident the others would follow his example. They did so in silence until, through the dusk, came Chalmers' unmistakable tones. He too had taken the sentry for a Frenchman and was giving his own version of '*Bonsoir, monsieur.*'

Thompson, who thought Broad must have been sleepwalking, hastened up to him, tugged at his arm and whispered, 'That was a Jerry sentry, sir!'

'Keep going. Keep going. Pay no attention. He's just a stupid Hun. He'll go away. Quicken your pace as I do.'

Gradually they pulled away, marching until at the first sign of dawn they piled into a ramshackle barn on the slopes below the coastal road.

Fatouville suffered the the problems that afflict places that are not on the road to anywhere. Its folk earned their living either by cutting timber on the wooded slopes or by rudimentary farming. The houses were scattered haphazardly round the church and *épicèrie* in a clearing on the plateau overlooking the not-too-distant shoreline. In its isolation it was not unlike some villages in East Anglia of which it was said the inhabitants all slept in the same bed and shared out the children at Christmas. The behaviour of some of its people was the despair of its curé.

Richard Broad's first impression of the place was coloured by the fact that when he called discreetly at a cottage the apparently sympathetic woman who produced the required bread and milk asked an extortionate price, strangers being fair game. With his 'shopping' experience of the past few days he was well aware of the cost of such things but had no alternative but to pay up.

Profiteer or not, she was the first contact he had made and, having shared the costly breakfast with his men, he returned by arrangement to the woman who was to guide him to the mayor. Broad's faith in authority remained unbroken at this stage of his adventures.

The lady did not lack confidence. She was certain they would not meet any Germans and therefore she was quite happy to walk down the road with him regardless of his British uniform. The mayor's house was some distance away and the journey proved to be in vain as he had gone to market. The couple retraced their steps. Not far from Fatouville a young man in blue overalls and a beret stopped in his tracks at the sight of them. Then he ran over and, switching his eyes from one to the other, began to talk rapidly. The woman flushed, muttered a reply, then made off. Broad was pulled into the shelter of the hedge and told in effect: 'What the hell do you think you're doing wandering about dressed like that? Don't you know the Germans have occupied the area?'

Military lorries and cars were constantly using the coast road and the N180 leading to Rouen.

The speaker, Raymond Lecesne, was probably the brightest spark in Fatouville. Dark and pale, at nineteen he had not been called up because of his health, but that did not prevent him from being fervently anti-German. There had been no problems with them so far, but he was on his guard. As for his own people he was afraid they might be deceived by the Germans. 'Trust no one,' he told Broad.

Lecesne made sure the road was clear before leading the Briton into the cover of trees near the hamlet. A betrayal by a Frenchman was unlikely, he explained. What was much more dangerous was the addiction of the locals to gossip. Someone was quite likely to talk too much, putting everyone, including themselves, at risk.

As the lad talked, Broad's confidence grew. This was the most serious helper he had met so far, cautious and intelligent. He revealed his hopes of getting a fishing boat in Honfleur to take the group to England.

Lecesne did not pretend that he could help immediately. From the beginning he thought this unlikely. The fishermen were not to be trusted. Living on the plateau he had the traditional suspicion of the men of the shore and the port. This did not mean that he would not try to help. Indeed he would cycle into Honfleur immediately and see what he might do. Later they might see Monsieur Bloom, 'un Anglais'.

Broad found the idea of an Englishman living near Fatouville hard to credit. Could he be someone of British extraction? From the name he might be Jewish and therefore in even greater danger from the Germans than he and his men.

The language difficulty prevented Lecesne putting over a credible explanation and Broad let the matter drop. He offered to accompany Lecesne into Honfleur but was told it was too risky. No civilian clothes could be found for him at such short notice. The young man cycled off alone and Broad returned to the men.

The Seaforths spent what can only be described as a social afternoon – one might even say an 'at home'. A constant stream of callers arrived at the door of the barn to stare and chatter. Thanks to the lady who had supplied the food, everyone had heard that eight British soldiers were encamped in the heart of Fatouville.

The great gossip herself appeared with a pat of butter and burst into tears as, undoubtedly stung by Lecesne's remarks, she returned the money she had extracted from Broad earlier. Politeness demanded that he accept her explanation that she had mistaken him for a German in disguise trying to trap her. Lecesne himself was back before long and reported that he had been unable to find any of the people he hoped might help. Soon afterwards the door of the barn opened yet again. A group of locals thrust forward a little old man in a black beret and blue working clothes and then stood back with unconcealed curiosity.

There had not been such a day in Fatouville since the last unmarried mother had twins. The little man stood uneasily for a moment, then spoke.

'Good afternoon.'

The accent was perfect.

'You must be Monsieur Bloom?'

'Not exactly. My name is really Blunt but they find it too difficult to pronounce around here.'

Blunt explained that his wife was French and that he had lived in the region for years after retiring from the Argentine railway service.

'Naturally the Germans keep a very close eye on me. I shouldn't be at all surprised if they send me off to a concentration camp one of these days. Meanwhile I'm just doing what I always do – fishing in the canal.'

He added that he would like to help but didn't see how he could, though he would go into Honfleur with Lecesne and see what could be done.

'At least tell us what's going on. I've heard nothing much since leaving St Valery.'

'I'm afraid you're not going to like it.'

He told how Italy had attacked in the Alps on 10 June, how the Germans had crossed the Loire, advanced deep into France and cut off the Maginot Line, and how Pétain had become the French leader and asked for an armistice. The radio predicted that it would be England's turn next. Frankly Blunt did not give Britain much hope. It was 'us against the rest' and he, for one, was not optimistic about the outcome.

'Monsieur Bloom' departed on his bicycle leaving his countrymen in reflective mood, all the more so because he was obviously sincere in his assessment of the situation. The French audience, noting the change in atmosphere, also departed. True to his word, Blunt returned that evening to report that he'd had no success in finding anyone willing to help with a boat. He would try again but . . .

Hope fell as he cycled off into the night but almost immediately more visitors arrived. Raymond Lecesne's mother ushered in two fishermen, one of them apparently engaged to a Lecesne girl. They thought they might be able to make the trip but they would have to wait for the rising wind to change and the sea to ease. It might take days.

The following morning in Fatouville saw the opening of a subtle psychological battle. Suddenly appreciating the danger they were in, the villagers decided to rid themselves of their uninvited guests; the Scots, still hopeful that the fishermen might come up trumps, did not feel like leaving their only source of contact, Raymond Lecesne.

The announcement that very day of the Franco-German armistice terms strengthened the resolve of the peasants. Even in Fatouville there were radios and copies of the local paper.

The most menacing news to come from the published details of the armistice talks was that Fatouville was in one of the zones designated for complete enemy domination, in which 'the German Reich exercises all the rights of an Occupying Power. The French Government obligates itself to support with every means the regulations resulting from the exercise of these rights and to carry them out with the aid of the French administration.'

Article 10 of the Armistice Agreement included the paragraph: 'The French Government will forbid French citizens to fight against Germany in the service of the States with which the German Reich is still at war. French citizens who violate this provision will be treated as insurgents.'

No one, least of all the citizens of Fatouville, had much doubt about what would happen to 'insurgents'. They might not have considered themselves as such, but it was clear that by aiding British soldiers they were in breach at least of the spirit of the Agreement, which, when all was said and done, had the backing of their own government. Throughout the day a succession of callers suggested to Broad that he and his men might move on and remove the threat to the whole village.

To the Scots, who had experience of previous attempts to get them to move on, it seemed that this time they ought to try staying put. The greater the anxiety felt by the locals the more they might try to find them a boat. In the meantime they were grateful to receive food from Raymond Lecesne's mother and did not wish to lose her support.

In the week that followed pressure was bought to bear on the Lecesnes. Apart from this added problem, they were a particularly poor family, the father having set up an equally humble establishment with another woman whom the Seaforths dubbed 'Drunken Annie'. Without financial help or general support from the neighbours, provision of food for the fugitives was a harsh burden. Raymond, ever helpful, found them another hideout which was more tumbledown than the first but which placed them further from the village.

Then the food supplies ceased. The lad, who had apparently been off work, had to go back and could not visit them during the day. With some embarrassment he pointed out that there was a café not far away and they might be able to buy supplies. The message was received and understood; the escapers did not blame young Lecesne.

The British as a whole can hardly be said to have endeared themselves to the French at this period. On 3 July the Royal Navy seized all French warships which had taken refuge in south coast ports, including a battleship, a light cruiser and destroyers and submarines at Portsmouth. Worse still, a British battle squadron had appeared off the great North African base of Mers el Kebir near Oran. When Admiral le Luc rejected demands for the neutralization of his force, *Hood*, *Resolution* and *Valiant* opened fire on the anchorage. Their 15-inch shells crashed down at the rate of twenty-four a minute. Of the French heavy ships, *Provence* caught fire and had to be beached, *Dunkerque* was badly damaged and immobilized and *Bretagne* drifted from the quay a mass of flames and blew up with the loss of more than a thousand of the crew. Only the new battle-cruiser *Strasbourg* reached the open sea and outdistanced her older assailants.

According to reports, two families from a village near Toulon, on the Mediterranean coast, who had each lost a son at Mers el Kebir agreed that the Union Jack should lie alongside the Tricolour when the bodies were brought home for burial. Nevertheless there was understandable bitterness. The towns along the Normandy coast traditionally supplied recruits to the navy. Why should anyone go out of their way to help save soldiers of a country which was so prodigal with French lives?

With the cessation of supplies at this time, Broad had to resort to his former practice of foraging with Turner each morning, not always with success. One friendly soul who gave them coffee sent off her grandson to do some shopping and he returned having spent most of the group's pooled exchequer on tins of tripe which they had no means of cooking. The old lady was thoroughly upbraided by the boy's mother when she arrived for putting them all at risk. As an excuse she said that she 'thought they were Germans'. Broad and Turner were asked to leave immediately.

'Drunken Annie' also got into the act, providing meagre groceries for which she overcharged.

At one point the Scots were driven to existing on red currants which flourished in an abandoned garden and made the interesting biological discovery that 'after a few days they seemed to lose all food value and indeed are not digested by the system at all'.

With no sign of fishermen with boats or any other means of escape, their prospects were looking bleak and the need to move was growing when the Jock on look-out duty reported a girl approaching. Fernande Lecesne, Raymond's sister, had been sent by the villagers to see if they had managed to starve out the Scots.

They made her as welcome as they could in their delapidated quarters. Ashamed of her own people, perhaps, she listened carefully as Broad explained that they quite understood how difficult it was for the families in Fatouville but pointed out that they were desperate for food. He asked her to take a note to 'Monsieur Bloom', who, he was sure, could help. In it he said that if the old man would accept a cheque he would see it was honoured at the earliest possible moment.*

* Broad did not have a cheque book but drew up his own cheques in a legal manner.

It was forbidden on pain of death to possess firearms, including sporting shotguns. Listening to the BBC was also *verboten* and jamming stations were set up to interfere with London's transmissions. Wireless enthusiasts were in great demand to find a way through the static, which they invariably did. A curfew applied between 10 pm and 6 am. No one could take up residence in the coastal zone without the permission of the *Kommandantur* and it was *verboten* to hold public meetings in the open air. Posters appeared saying it was *verboten* even to count the German aircraft flying over Honfleur to bomb Britain.

By contrast it was obligatory to report to the occupation forces all Allied parachute landings (meaning at that time shot-down airmen) and the whereabouts of any Allied soldiers.

Lists of hostages were compiled, to be seized and executed if reprisals were required for attacks on the occupying forces. Oppressive racial laws were introduced as far as Honfleur was concerned in a region where anti-Semitism had previously been unknown.

Three other measures rubbed salt into deep and painful wounds. From the first day of the armistice the exchange rate of the Franc was raised from 12 to 20 to the Deutschmark; France had to observe German summertime; and only the swastika flag was permitted on German-occupied buildings.

To enforce their rule the Nazis recruited auxiliaries from French fascist organizations. Within eighteen months of the armistice there were fifteen police or para-military police forces operating in the country. To add to the confusion of not knowing whom one could trust, the far Left had become as suspect as the far Right. The Russo-German non-aggression pact of 1939 meant, on the face of it, that French communists were obliged to perform a swift about-turn. With the press controlled by the *Propaganda staffel* it was almost impossible to tell fact from fiction. From the heart of a population floundering in suspicion, resentment and ignorance, Broad had to extricate seven stolid soldiers. It was a tall order and the problems grew worse as the time passed.

There was every indication that the Germans knew there were still a number of British soldiers in hiding in Northern France. Bailleul, leaving home one morning, found himself face to face with a poster which stated that after a particular date anyone found to be sheltering British soldiers or German deserters would automatically face the death sentence. Detective Bellanger, whose wife * worked as an interpreter at

---

* Madame Bellanger provided valuable information to the Resistance throughout the war.

the *Kommandantur*, obtained a copy of the poster for the Commissaire. Bailleul brought it home wrapped round a bunch of flowers for his wife. It was her saint's day, 19 August.

To Maria Bailleul it seemed quite unreal. She had spent much of the afternoon teaching Broad to make mayonnaise.

The little French nun and the English mule had far to go and it was not one of the mule's going days. Stubbornly he pulled to the left. Firmly Soeur Marie-Gabriel tugged his bit to the right. The Duchemin-Georgettes were farmers and she was not going to let down the family name. The couple proceeded on an erratic course. A strange animal this mule – dark beige in colour, he was usually tractable and sure-footed, despite his addiction to Anglo-Saxon road rules. On this occasion he seemed sulky and resentful of the company they were keeping. There were ten German soldiers cycling in front of the cart and about the same number trailing along in the rear. It was, Soeur Marie-Gabriel conceded, just the weather for a spin, though she would have preferred to travel alone. She was on her way to the château of Pennedepie to sound out the owner, Mme Revillon, on the chances of providing a hideout for the Seaforths if necessary, though ostensibly her task was to solicit supplies for the hospital. She was in no hurry. Nor was the mule or, it seemed, the Germans. As if disgusted with their presence *Le Mulet* – he was never given a name but always referred to simply as *Le Mulet* – fell on his knees. Soeur Marie-Gabriel dismounted and urged him to rise. The Germans paused to watch.

Soon after the march to Pennedepie had been resumed the obstinate animal slumped to his knees again. A brown and white figure shot over his head and rolled in the dust. The nun was assisted to her feet by some of her Wehrmacht escort and half a dozen of them heaved the mule to his feet. His knees bloody and bruised, he trudged glumly on, still hanging to the left.

The nun's mission was in vain. The heir to Pennedepie was flying with the Royal Air Force and, to make his family aware of their displeasure, the Germans had quartered an anti-aircraft battery in the grounds of the château.

It had been Soeur Marie-Gabriel's intention to visit the Lusts and Madame Morin that day but the state of *Le Mulet's* legs and her own bumps and bruises required a return to the convent. The Germans, keeping a kindly eye on her, cycled part of the way before tailing off.

The next time the little nun received the close attention of the Germans was late on a September evening. Lorries pulled up outside the convent and troops leaped out and surrounded the area. Men in steel helmets carrying rifles and bayonets clumped up the Rue Alphonse Allais and took up positions outside the hospital.

Three main buildings were involved in the search – the hospital, which provided the usual medical facilities for a small French town; the hospice, which housed a hundred chronically sick old men and women; and the convent, which supplied the nursing staff for the hospice. The head of the amalgam as far as administration was concerned was a civilian director, Monsieur Fortin, a hardworking man quite unaware of the connection between his establishment and certain clandestine activities in the area.

He was outraged when the troops arrived and he complained bitterly as they tramped through the wards staring hard at all the male patients, sometimes asking for their papers. He became quite voluble when they insisted on entering the hospice. He knew nothing of the battledress blouses hanging in the wardrobe full of the black Sunday suits of peasants past and present, nor of the equipment stored in sacks in the loft. But the Germans were not looking for weapons, or evidence of Allied soldiers. They were looking for a man, or perhaps men. As they lined up the nuns for some mild questioning – the Germans included a number of Catholics from Saxony – their quarry was actually watching them. Broad was on the terrace of the Bailleul's home. Two night's earlier and he would have been inside the convent.

Broad had spent almost a week in the convent while Maria Bailleul was in Paris. She had gone there in the second week of September, 1940, to try to contact Jean Borotra, a distant relative. She had heard that he had helped a Jewish family to flee the country and wondered if he might be able to help. On learning that he had accepted a post in the Vichy government and was in the Unoccupied Zone, she kept her own counsel and returned home.

Broad had thoroughly enjoyed his stay at the convent, where he had been given a room. He spent his time knitting and copying music in the Mother Superior's lounge. From it he could watch the shipping on the Seine estuary and study the aerial activity generated by the Battle of Britain.

The night after Maria Bailleul returned to Honfleur the Mother Superior invited her to dinner with her husband and Broad returned to No. 1 Rue de Baudelaire afterwards.

The next day, Friday the 13th, passed without incident. On Saturday Madame Pignet, the local *sage-femme*, joined the Bailleuls for the evening meal. The good-looking midwife was a valuable ally of the Commissaire. Her duties enabled her to travel throughout the region at all hours. She picked up much information as she went to and fro ushering little Honfleurais into a troubled world. It was also easy for her to carry messages to either the Lusts or Madame Morin.

As Bailleul showed his guest out after dinner, he found himself face to face with an armed German sentry at the door leading into the Rue Alphonse Allais. On production of her pass Madame Pignet was allowed to cycle off. Bailleul hurried back to warn Broad that there were soldiers all round the place. From the roof terrace both men carefully watched the proceedings.

The Mother Superior was an early visitor to No. 1 Rue de Baudelaire on Sunday morning. She was highly agitated and said the Germans had agreed not to search the convent only after she had given her word that no English soldiers were hidden there.* The real problem was that an informer was at work, almost certainly one of the doctors who was an avowed communist. Once again the Russo-German non-aggression pact was bearing fruit. Perhaps he had become suspicious because there had been a hunt for men's shoes in the hospice, or maybe he had heard whispers in Honfleur. It was now obvious that the Germans had not followed Soeur Marie-Gabriel by accident when she went with *Le Mulet* † to Pennedepie. The nun had remembered coming across the doctor on his bicycle once or twice on previous trips. Perhaps he had followed her to the Lusts' and Madame Morin's. Was it significant that the search had taken place only two days after Broad had stayed in the convent? Or was it coincidence?

Though the presence in the area of British soldiers was known to only a handful of nuns, the search had made them nervous. The doctor was not going to take kindly to being made a fool of. It was in everyone's interests for Broad to move and new hideouts to be found for the others forthwith.

---

* She was told by the German officer that he would not search the Convent if she gave her word that they were not harbouring English soldiers. She gave this assurance, because, as she said, they were not, after all, English but Scottish. Later she went to Confessional to obtain absolution for her white lie.

† The mule survived the war and was a common sight in Honfleur for some time afterwards, still pulling to the left.

XIII

Love and Blackmail

'Marité, we have a problem.'

The greying woman so addressed nodded understandingly and said, 'Ah, yes.'

It was a period when a lot of people had a lot of problems. She did not trifle with glances but gave Broad a cool questioning stare.

Francette Joba went on.

'We need your help.'

'We?'

Another stare.

'This is Richard. He is a British officer.'

'I think you had better come in.'

Broad waded through a milling pack of large, hairy dogs into a room dominated by oil paintings, dark timber and art nouveau stained glass windows. Not all the dogs were house-trained, he decided.

'So you want me to hide your officer?'

'Please.'

'All right. Though I'm afraid I can't offer him any lunch at the moment.'

'There's something else. There may be one or two others. At least three this afternoon.'

'Of course.'

'Marité, there could be some more this evening.'

Mademoiselle Marie-Thérèse Turgis, then about 40, was one of the characters of the Côte de Grâce; among other things she smoked a pipe. When younger she had shocked the staid little town of Pont

Audemer, some miles along the Honfleur-Rouen road, by running away with an artist called Leclerc. Together they had built the house on an isolated part of the Côte, lavishing a great deal of love on the buildings and the garden. Then Monsieur Leclerc had died and Marie-Thérèse had been left alone to carry on with her painting, her sculpture, her garden and her dogs. Two of the powerful Briards regularly pulled her in a small cart to Honfleur to do her shopping.

The dogs helped her to maintain her privacy, though she was far from being a recluse. Well read and informed, she held strong opinions. As she did not approve of the Treaty of Versailles she had not spoken English – in which she was fluent – since the signing in June, 1919; though as the French had also signed it her attitude was not altogether logical.

When the Germans overran Normandy, Mademoiselle Turgis was in the Dordogne. She was not impressed by what she found on her return home. The Manoir du Parc had been searched by the Germans in her absence and they had left it in a mess. One picture, undoubtedly considered 'decadent' art, had been slashed and magazines containing anti-Nazi articles had been ripped and lay scattered about the floor. There might well have been more damage but the officer who supervised the search took it on himself to write a letter answering the points made in the offending articles. It was rather dignified, if unconvincing. The day Richard Broad arrived Marie-Thérèse Turgis began, somewhat rustily, to speak English again.

The three Scots from the Lust farm arrived without incident that afternoon, whereupon, having greeted them, Mademoiselle Turgis departed to take tea at the Bois Normand. Broad warned Nicole, who had joined the party, not to attempt to transfer the other soldiers from Madame Morin's until he was present, and remained to explore the new hideout and settle in the men. He could have saved his breath. Marité returned to say that the girls were intent on bringing the other men and they did so in the evening, having guided them across the fields.

Nicole had scouted ahead, signalling that the coast was clear by hooting like an owl. Broad was not amused, though, as the girls knew the area well, they were probably better equipped than he to do the job. It was the element of mischief in their action that worried him most. They were apt to be too exuberant. Calling at Bailleul's house on one occasion they had rung 'SOS' on the doorbell, not realizing that it would send Broad racing for cover in the loft and Maria Bailleul frantically clearing away all evidence of a lodger. Not surprisingly the 'humour' of the occasion had escaped the long-suffering Commissaire.

The Manoir du Parc stood in its own grounds about fifty yards from the road which led from the Chapelle de Nôtre Dame. Next to the double gates was a kennel block occupied by sundry Briards whose appearance and noise were calculated to deter snoopers, particularly as one or two dogs were frequently at liberty. A thick shrubbery of rhododendrons dominated by a monkey puzzle tree screened the approach to the creeper-clad house. Behind it the customary wooded ravines ran down to the sea. The Bois Normand was only a matter of minutes away to the east along the same road; a German headquarters was rather further away at La Roche Vasouy to the west. The Côte also housed other military installations and a flak battery was deployed in Madame Morin's fields shortly after the Scots left.

A major crisis arose when Nicole announced that one of her unmarried maids was pregnant. Mademoiselle Turgis's eyebrows rose sharply. She removed her pipe from her mouth to pour forth a torrent of questions. Nicole thought that a German orderly was to blame, but the maid was going to tell the Germans that Broad had been staying there unless Nicole kept her on instead of sending her to Bayeux, where there was a home run by nuns for girls in her position.

Nicole made it plain that, war or no war, she was not prepared to keep the miserable girl under her roof a moment longer than was necessary. For a single girl to become pregnant was bad enough. For a single girl to have a baby by a German was an extremely unhappy state of affairs. Nicole went on to say that the girl was also asking for money.

Some quick thinking was called for. Broad had taken great pains to ensure that the whereabouts of the Jocks was known only to a select few, and therefore the girl did not know where anyone else was. So she could tell the Germans nothing useful. Therefore they decided to wait.

While they did so the unhappy Monsieur Bouchet de Fareins, back from his factory again, was confronted with the problem and stated gloomily that he had known something like this was bound to happen. His solution was to pay the girl off, which he did.

Unhappily he gave her a cheque, thus providing her with evidence of something or other.

The situation began to assume worrying proportions. Supposing the girl did go to the Germans and they decided to investigate, they might well put pressure on the other maid to talk, or the man who helped with the garden, or Madame Joba.

The stumbling block was the insistence of Nicole that the girl would have to leave her service. The girl was just as adamant that she would not go into a religious refuge to have her baby, such establishments having the reputation of being far from comfortable. Contrition and repentance were obligatory.

No one knows exactly what went on when the girl finally went to the *Kommandantur* but it seems that the German officer concerned was a student of human nature. The story seemed incredible. Besides, didn't everyone know that girls in a certain condition were apt to have flights of fancy? Then there was her evident fear of the nuns' régime at Bayeux. The suggestion that British soldiers were moving out virtually as the Germans moved in was just too preposterous for words. The officers billeted in the Bois Normand had nothing but praise for their quarters. The owner's wife was rather icy but that was understandable. Her husband seemed to have been most generous to the girl. These French would have to get used to the fact that, human nature being what it was, the romance of the maid and the German soldier was not going to be unique in this war.

Despite the proximity of so many Germans, Broad always felt at home in the Manoir du Parc. Basic worries were diminishing. Food had now ceased to be his major problem. The Lusts, only a short distance away, were able to supply farm produce. Edmond Bailleul, by virtue of the fact that he worked in the Mairie building, was able to supply blank ration cards and obtain food coupons which he 'borrowed' when he was working late.

Marité's house was comfortable, with the Jocks sleeping in a former studio and Broad able to have a mattress, supplied by Maria Bailleul, all to himself. Marité did the cooking and the men helped with the chores and chopped wood for the stove.

Eight men were just too many to cope with, however, and when the excitement died down Osborne, McDonagh and Turner returned to the Lusts and Drayton and Dodd eventually went to Fatouville and Madame Lecesne. The return of Madame Morin's husband, on whom the Germans might be expected to check now and again as a discharged soldier, made the use of La Valoreine too dangerous.

Pleasant as life was at the Manoir du Parc, where Marité would burn a selection of fragrant twigs in the evenings, sometimes waving them under the noses of the fascinated Jocks, it was not without its excitements.

Everyone had a job to do and it was Thompson's duty to rake out the ashes from the wood stove each morning, put them into a bucket to cool and then dump them in a trench used for rubbish. One day, for reasons best known to himself, Thompson decided that waiting for the ashes to cool was a waste of time and disposed of the lot under the nearest clump of rhododendrons. That night was a peaceful one at the Manoir du Parc. Marité was smoking her pipe, Broad was knitting – a skill he had developed under the tuition of various ladies – and Thompson and Chalmers were playing *jaquet*, a French version of backgammon. Then the smouldering bonfire exploded.

Suddenly the doors rattled, and switching off the light, the Scots ran out and found the rhododendrons ablaze. Mademoiselle Turgis screamed, the dogs barked furiously and the soldiers ran for water. Through the anguished cries of his 'landlady', the yelping of the Briards and the hissing of the embers, Thompson learned what Broad thought of him. An outraged Mademoiselle Turgis retired with her dogs for the night but the Seaforths had to 'stand to' for unwelcome callers, ready to bolt to pre-arranged hiding places in the woods.

A drill to use on the arrival of doubtful visitors had been worked out well in advance. Because of the stained glass windows outsiders could not see into the studio the men used as their quarters. An external door led from it to the garden and the wood beyond. This was kept shut and the Jocks had strict instructions to open it to no one. It was solely for emergencies. One snowy day the sisters from the Bois Normand decided to test the system, creeping quietly round the rear of the house. They knocked hard. Silence. They knocked again and on the other side Chalmers sidled out to tell Broad, who was helping Marité in the kitchen.

By this time the cold had begun to take the edge off the joke and Nicole called out in a deep voice the name she best remembered: 'Thompson, Thompson!'

The tough little regular was not one to shirk responsibility. Marching to the door he called, 'I'se not ben let youse in!'

That he thought had disposed of the matter and he was quite indignant when Broad ticked him off yet again.

Such incidents were small beer by comparison with the near threat which loomed at Fatouville.

Dodd and Drayton had settled in nicely with Madame Lecesne,

next door to the Bruyères. They slept in a loft which they entered by leaping from the ground straight into a door on the gable end – a door through which hay had been hoisted for storage in earlier days. Each had a bed of chicken wire stretched on frames on either side of the chimney breast. It was as good as central heating. They got plenty of exercise working with Bruyère and anyone not in the know would have been mystified at the way in which Madame Lecesne's garden would be dug apparently overnight – which was exactly what happened.

To help out with the food supply Dodd resorted to catching rabbits, a knack he had picked up as a boy, and was able to provide three or four a week. He and Drayton even went into business in a small way, digging worms on the shore below Fatouville which Raymond sold to the local fishermen. Both found girlfriends locally, introduced by the Lecesnes. Of the worm trade and the girlfriends they said nothing to Broad.

They learned to knit, Fernande and Janine starting them off on producing squares which eventually they made into blankets. Though they were given magazines they were of little use once they had studied the pictures and they whiled away the hours when it was too dangerous to circulate by arguing about anything, literally anything at all. The respective merits of Crewe as a railway centre as opposed to Doncaster (being respectively near the homes of Dodd and Drayton) absorbed hours of conversation. Occasionally Soeur Marie-Gabriel made a contact visit and had to hauled up through the hay loft door. They enjoyed their attempts at conversation with her and even taught her to play pontoon, if not exactly how to win. Not all her visits were to be social.

The pain came on unexpectedly and was excruciating. Dodd sat down heavily on the rickety bed and great drops of sweat spattered the floor.

Madame Lecesne felt Dodd's brow and studied him anxiously. When another paroxysm seized him she fetched one of the girls. Dodd could make out the word '*appendicite*' and didn't need to have it translated. He began to figure out the options. They seemed to lie between giving himself up immediately or giving himself up later – unless the attack eased off. Then there was a third option – he could 'pop his clogs'. The appendix would burst and finish him off with peritonitis.

Broad was appalled when he received the news and hurried over. If this were an acute appendix case the only way to save Dodd would be to operate and there was only one hospital where that could be done.

He began to work out possible schemes, think up cover stories. After the months that had passed since the fall of France it would be useless for Dodd to pretend he had hidden out on his own. The Mother Superior would have to be consulted.

In his extremity Dodd was prepared to try anything but he found it hard to believe the obnoxious potion brought by little Soeur Marie-Gabriel could ease his suffering. True, she had examined him in expert fashion before disappearing to fetch a large jar containing granulated black powder. But she was no doctor. Dodd regarded the sooty table-spoon with considerable misgivings. It looked like charcoal and those who professed to know the flavour of charcoal sampled it and said it was.

Dodd took nearly two hours to consume the contents of the spoon. It almost choked him if he tried to swallow it too quickly, and left a taste he equated with coal dust which lingered for hours. But it worked. The pain eased. He recovered.

The Lecesnes reckoned that Soeur Marie-Gabriel's prayers had much to do with saving his life. The medical explanation was that the young nun had correctly diagnosed an intestinal inflammation and had selected the right treatment – formocarbine – from the pharmacy at the hospital. In Drayton's opinion Dodd was too mean to die before he had made it back to England and drawn his back pay, which by then amounted to quite a sum.

This was not the only time that *la petite soeur* used her healing touch on the Scots. When two of the others went down with slight touches of pneumonia she drew out the inflammation with *ventuses* * and mustard plaster. Broad comforted the patients with the news that the bumps and bruises on their backs made them resemble black and white hedgehogs.

Towards the end of 1940 money became tight. Through Bailleul, people like the Boucherot brothers and Monsieur Duchêne, the cautious mayor of Honfleur, had helped considerably, but Broad felt that he could not expect to live on charity for ever. When Nicole announced that she was taking two of her children to visit a Paris dentist he gave her a letter from the head of the Guaranty Trust, an American bank with which he had had dealings before the war. It was a simple request for financial assistance but was to have far-reaching results.

* *Ventuses*: glass cups heated with cotton wool and methylated spirits clamped on the spot to draw out inflammation.

Under the circumstances Christmas and New Year proved to be unusually festive for Snow White and the Seven Dwarfs. At Fatouville, with the girl's help, Dodd and Drayton had managed to knit pullovers as presents for the Lecesnes. They also overhauled and painted the family's bicycles, carefully heeding a warning from Monsieur 'Bloom' to copy a French colour scheme and not one typically English. For the baby in the house they produced a rag doll.

There was a novel problem at the Manoir du Parc during the school holidays. Two grandsons of the historian Albert Sorel, whose bust dominates the centre of Honfleur, proved to be very inquisitive. Though staying with the Bouchet de Fareins, they were frequent callers at the Manoir where they had been used to having the run of the house. The locked door behind which the Seaforths were hidden merely excited their curiosity and Broad decided in the end it would be easier to take the lads into their confidence. It was the sort of adventure boys dream of and they kept their secret until the liberation.

Visiting the Lusts on Christmas Eve, Broad found the three refugees puffing cigars provided by the non-smoking farmer and enjoying a good meal.

On New Year's Eve all eight of the Seaforths were reunited at the Manoir du Parc, twelve-year-old André Lust guiding the three soldiers across the fields from his father's farm.

Sergeant Chalmers had quietly arranged for all uniforms to be collected and spruced up. Broad was called to the front door on some pretext and found the men lined up in battledress. Chalmers' great moment came when he was able to announce: 'Sir, the Second Battalion the Seaforth Highlanders present and ready for your inspection, Sir!'

An improvised Athol Brose, a traditional regimental drink with a potent spirit base, was then served to all present, including the two sisters from the Bois Normand.

There was much discussion of the Boucherot petrol tanker escape plan that night. Broad did not dream that within a matter of days he would be in Paris.

XIV
Jodhpurs Princess

Josh Campbell, manager of the Guaranty Trust's Paris Office, had been wary of the young woman who brought the letter. He told her she had been reckless to hide eight British soldiers, but he did not refuse point-blank to help. He said the regulations of the bank made it impossible for him to advance any cash but he had a client who might be helpful. If she would return the following day . . .

The next morning Nicole learned that the client had been informed and was going to pass on the request to a young relative who had connections with possible sympathizers. When he had further news he would advise her that her 'appointment with the dentist' had been arranged and she would have to call on him again.

Soon after the New Year Campbell's letter arrived and Nicole returned to Paris. A slim, bespectacled young man whom she later described in Honfleur as '*très distingué*', was waiting to meet her.

The affair was about to assume, at least for a while, very aristocratic overtones. To start with the client to whom Campbell had referred turned out to be Prince André Poniatowski. The family numbered Polish kings among their ancestors and were related to the Napoleonic marshal of that name who drowned while trying to swim his horse across the Elster following the Emperor's defeat at Leipzig. This connection may not have been the best omen for other would-be-escapers from a lost battle!

Prince André had called in a nephew, Comte Pierre d'Harcourt, to look into Campbell's problem.

Très distingué Comte Pierre might have been but he had not risen above the rank of *soldat deuxième classe* during his service. As it is the custom of French officers to address the lower ranks paternally as 'thou' this was a source of irritation to them. Such familiarity was unthinkable with a d'Harcourt, second-class or not. Thus his squad might be heard being addressed by a corporal or a second-lieutenant, '*Tu Lejeune, tu Dubost, tu Mabire et vous d'Harcourt*'.

The d'Harcourts had warlike roots. They could claim to have fought on both sides at Agincourt and over the centuries a battle had hardly been worthy of the name if one of them did not feature in the casualty lists. No one was surprised when Pierre d'Harcourt was captured during the battle for the Channel ports in 1940.

Pierre d'Harcourt was not a prisoner long. He determined to escape from the military hospital where he was working as an orderly. Among the patients was one Captain Airey Neave, a Royal Engineers officer, captured at Calais. Neave, lying wounded, wanted to know what an 'able-bodied young man like you is doing in a place like this?'

Unabashed, d'Harcourt replied that he was just a 'travelling nurse' and invited Neave to join in the escape bid. The Briton declined.

Not long afterwards d'Harcourt reached Paris, was officially de-mobilized and proceeded to find means for carrying on the battle. He later recalled his uncle, Prince Jean de Caraman Chimay, head of the Veuve Cliquot champagne firm, wrapping the Tricolour round some of the younger members of the family and swearing they would all be *resistants*.

It is hardly surprising that another of the brood, Prince Alphonse de Chimay, Comte de Caraman, was serving as a major in the Middlesex Regiment at the time.

Pierre d'Harcourt, despite his total commitment to the Resistance, was an agent of the Vichy intelligence service, but not an ordinary one. His superiors were behind a highly secret section set up to pass in-formation to the British. The trouble with this secret service within a secret service was that their contacts with the British were very limited. To the astonishment of the anti-Nazi officers the *Services Spéciaux*, their former allies had left no links behind – no professional agents. As far as they were aware they had not left so much as a radio. Contacts had to be made through the laborious system of contacting embassies in neutral countries, or through the Americans.

The need for increased liaison was urgent and the pro-British element in Vichy were naturally most interested in an officer who had managed to remain in the midst of Occupied France for so long without being detected – especially if he had the right qualifications.

Initially Broad was a disappointment to d'Harcourt. He had travelled to Honfleur with another agent, causing Nicole some concern, as the stranger was introduced only as 'Paoli' and she feared some sort of trap. Finally persuaded that both her visitors were genuine, she gave them dinner. The presence of the Germans billeted in the house did not spoil their appetites and afterwards they all went to the Manoir du Parc.

Somehow d'Harcourt had gained the impression that Broad was fluent in French and it took only a few words of conversation to realize that his knowledge of the language was only basic. However, after a long discussion the visitors agreed to take Broad back to Paris with them to see if there was any way in which the little band of escapers could be extricated. Being legitimate guests, having supplied themselves with all the necessary papers, d'Harcourt and 'Paoli' re-entered the Bois Normand by the front door. Broad sneaked in by the open window and the invaluable ladder. The following morning he crept out and joined his companions on a train packed with Germans. It was his first journey by public transport since the battalion had steamed into the bombed station yard at Rouen.

The journey was filled with danger and Broad felt that at any time a hand would descend upon his shoulder, or he would feel the barrel of a gun in his back. The worst moment came when a scuffle broke out among some soldiers and spilled over to where he was standing while waiting to go to the lavatory. He fell to the ground and such was his surprise that he let out a very English-sounding expletive. He found himself looking up into the eyes of a hard-faced military policeman, who picked him up and pinned him against the lavatory door. The German stared into Broad's eyes with a quizzical look and was about to speak to him when his attention was attracted by a renewed outbreak of fighting behind him. He released Broad and turned to confront the trouble, whereupon Broad took the opportunity to slip away. He spent the rest of the journey hidden behind the pages of a magazine, hardly daring to turn the pages.

Paris in January, 1941, was a sad, hungry place. The Nazi mask was beginning to slip. From the day the armistice was signed Hitler began to gear the French economy to support his war effort. Almost a quarter of the country's steam locomotives were requisitioned (some 40,000), along with half France's freight cars. Thousands of horses were seized and more than 10 percent of all agricultural produce was sent to the Reich. Bakers gained some small pleasure from turning away German officers' wives who arrived on holiday seeking cream gâteaux which no longer existed. The sale of alcohol was also controlled, being available in bars and restaurants on alternate days only. Those on the run did well to remember which was a '*jour avec*' and which a '*jour sans*'. A slip could draw attention to them, as no resident Frenchman was likely to forget such a vital piece of information.

In September, 1940, the bread ration was reduced to nine ounces with half an ounce of fat a day. The weekly allowance of meat and cheese was six-and-a-half ounces and one-and-a-half ounces respectively. The monthly sugar ration was seventeen-and-a-half ounces. Instead of an intake of 3,200 calories, generally regarded as necessary for good health, the French had to make do with 1,800 calories. Later this fell further.

More than a million French soldiers were still held in Germany as prisoners of war and anyone contemplating acts of resistance had to bear these hostages in mind.

The curfew varied. Normally imposed at 11 pm, it could be extended to midnight as a concession. Alternatively it could be imposed much earlier as a punishment. Paris, like the rest of the Occupied Zone, was at the mercy of the German military governor.

The Metro services were reduced and there were few vehicles about the streets of the capital. Petrol-driven cars were certain to contain either Germans, collaborators or some essential user like a doctor. Occasionally one saw *gazogènes*, cars powered by wood gas manufactured by a small furnace at the rear to fill a balloon-like container on the roof. Instead of cabs there were velo-taxis – hefty bicycles towing wickerwork panniers for two. The only booming business was the black-market.

On their arrival in Paris Broad's companions spent some time trying to phone a particular contact to arrange accommodation. They had no success so decided to have lunch in a restaurant full of German officers. Broad felt distinctly uncomfortable but 'Paoli', a tall, tough-looking man, seemed completely at ease, laughing and joking throughout the meal. As, on leaving, they collected their coats from the cloakroom his high spirits carried him away. On hearing Broad say '*merci*' to the hat-check girl he leaned over the counter, beaming, and said, '*On ne dit pas merci, aujourd hui. On dit Bardia!*' News had just come through that the North African fortress had fallen and the Italian army had been routed. One or two French diners, overhearing, laughed spontaneously but the Germans did not seem to notice.

The afternoon was spent trudging round Paris in between phone calls before d'Harcourt eventually got through. Princesse Jacqueline de Broglie would be happy to receive them that evening.

'Paoli' having gone his own way, Broad and his companion dined in a restaurant on the Champs Élysées where the staff were sympathetic but indiscreet. Perhaps his strange garb attracted attention; he was wearing an ill-fitting black polo-necked sweater which when pulled down at the front rose at the back and vice-versa. Then again, it might have been his accent. The head waiter, overhearing some conversation, told one of his minions in a clear voice: 'Don't forget the potatoes English style (*pommes de terre anglaises*).' To Broad's horror the band struck up a popular English tune during the meal: 'Any umbrellas . . . any umbrellas to mend today?' In France that had been the signature tune of Neville Chamberlain! He was relieved when it was time to go.

From the Champs Élysées to Neuilly was quite a walk. They crossed the Étoile and passed the Abwehr headquarters in the Avenue Foch just west of the Arc de Triomphe and eventually arrived in Paris's most fashionable suburb. A wall surrounded the house of Daisy Fellowes, mother of Jacqueline de Broglie, in the Rue St James and d'Harcourt pressed a bell and waited for the caretaker to open the door by remote control.

Broad was able to slip in quickly in the darkness, and stood by the wall while d'Harcourt entered openly and spoke to the caretaker.

Broad could hardly complain about the society he was obliged to keep. Jacqueline de Broglie's father, Prince Jean, had been killed in the First World War. Her mother, a daughter of the Duc Decazes, called Daisy by her friends, had married a friend of the Duke of Windsor, the Hon Reginald Fellowes. She had fled to England on the fall of France, but Princess Jacqueline, a French citizen, had remained and was working as a nurse at the American Hospital at Neuilly. Broad wondered if the Germans knew that she was a goddaughter of Winston Churchill.

The Princess entered the room wearing jodhpurs and clutching a black puppy, which she had said she was trying to housetrain. Having got used to the casual habits of the massive Briards at the Manoir du Parc, Broad felt confident that he would be able to put up with any

* Bardia in Gyrenaica, fell to 6th Australian Division and 7th Armoured Division on 4 January, 1941.

inconvenience the tiny animal might cause. As he sat chatting and sipping a scotch before a bright fire in the studio where he was to sleep he reflected that it was a far cry from the mattress he had been happy to use not so long before in Monsieur Bruyère's rabbit shed. Better still, Broad and the Princess had mutual acquaintances. Harcourt Gold, one of the partners in Broad's stockbroking firm, was a close friend of Reggie Fellowes. That sort of connection helped.

The following morning, with the entry of a manservant carrying his breakfast tray – the Broglie household did not go short of butter and eggs – Broad decided it was the sort of war one could get used to. Unfortunately it was not to last. Having bumped into the Princess's elderly aunt on the stairs as he emerged from the bathroom he politely said, 'Good morning'. The good lady fled. Soon afterwards Jacqueline de Broglie informed her guest that the domestic staff had mutinied. Either the Englishman left the house or they did. She was sorry but . . .

Pierre d'Harcourt, who was staying with his uncle, Count Bernard de Francqueville, in the Rue Elisée Reclus at the time, took Broad there. He spent only one night, however. It was deemed too risky to remain longer.

Jacqueline de Broglie eventually found Broad a room in what was virtually an accommodation hostel for the American Hospital, a large house a little distance away where doctors and nurses stayed, generally after they had been on late duty. One of the nurses, an Australian called Betty O'Neil, had been interned by the Germans and, though she was expecting to be released at any moment, her room was available. To the owner of the house, who was referred to by all and sundry simply as 'Lanova', Jacqueline de Broglie explained that Broad was a neutral Irishman who had to lie low from the Germans for a while. This seemed to be acceptable and Broad moved in. With comings and goings at all times of the day and night he would hardly be noticed. Nor was the language problem so acute.

These arrangements took time, however, and it was dark by the time they were complete. The Princess did not feel safe walking home on her own so Broad had to escort her back to the Rue St James, praying in his turn that he would be able to find his way back to his new hideout. The return trip took him some time and after the exertions of the day he had no difficulty in falling asleep. Hardly had he put his head down, it seemed, when he was roused by cheerful Australian tones. The room's authentic occupant was back from internment and it looked as though Broad would be moving again.

The lame story about being an Irishman did not seem to be at all convincing and Broad decided that it would be fairer to disclose his true identity. As a released internee Betty O'Neil was quite likely to be checked on by the police, and his presence, if detected, might have serious consequences. He would quite understand if she wanted him to leave.

Betty 'Boop', as she was nicknamed, was made of stern stuff, however, and would not hear of his departure. She thought it prudent, nevertheless, to conceal the truth from Lanova.

With a feeling of relief at having a firm base, Broad turned his thoughts to the business in hand, unaware of the trouble his presence was causing elsewhere.

Captain Jacques d'Autrevaux, to whom Pierre d'Harcourt and 'Paoli' reported on their return to Paris, had problems enough on his mind without having to worry about the travel arrangements for eight itinerant British soldiers. The French Army's intelligence service, to which he belonged, had taken little notice of the terms of the Armistice. The day after it was signed Colonel Rivet, head of the Special Services, had calmly drawn up a charter for a new organization – 'the struggle continues whatever may happen'.

A professional soldier and veteran of the First World War, d'Autrevaux had been recalled from the Reserve and given the command of a cavalry squadron in 1939. Early the following year he joined the Deuxième Bureau of the Second Army and, when France fell was serving in the Services Spéciaux. Under the direction of Captain Léon Simoneau working from a secret headquarters in Vichy, he had been sent to Paris to 'pick up the pieces' of the service and establish a clandestine intelligence-gathering organization. By August of that year it was in operation. A constant flow of reports was being sent to Simoneau for assessment and onward transmission to British and American contacts. Helping itinerant British soldiers to escape was not part of the programme.

The choice lay between sentiment and stern duty. Fully appreciating the desire of his agents to see the 'English' on their way – and success would give a wonderful boost to morale – d'Autrevaux had other factors to consider. If his men were involved in an irrelevant task even for two or three days, it would seriously weaken his operations. If the escapers were caught and the organization 'blown' the consequences would be disastrous.

All of these things he had to weigh against the arguments of his young subordinates. Finally he gave his consent on the understanding that no time would be wasted.

From a logical point of view all concerned knew they had no business to become involved with escapers but the temptation was great and, like d'Harcourt, 'Paoli' was desperate to do something – almost anything – to strike at the Nazis.

XV

'Quoi? Alors! Comment!'

Captain Jacques Robert was not the surrendering sort. During the
fighting at Rethel in mid-May, 1940, his platoon of three tanks had
accounted for thirty Panzers and armoured vehicles.* He had also
taken part in the French 2nd Armoured Division's attack on the
Abbeville bridgehead, when the Highlanders were committed in June.
He had then been moved to the Loire where he heard the first news of
Pétain's request for an armistice over the radio of a Char B-1. Forthwith
he decided it did not apply to him.

Taking himself off to Vichy to explore the lie of the land he tracked
down Simoneau in an office in the Boulevard des États Unis and asked
him bluntly, 'Whose side are you really on?'

'Why the British, of course!'

And that was that. 'Paoli' was born.† More than six feet tall and
physically powerful, Robert, who had been a successful businessman
before the war, possessed great charm. He was charming to the stout
Comtesse de Chambon whom he met over dinner at the Hôtel du Parc
(where Marshal Pétain had his office). He was charming to her husband, General de Chambon. He was even charming to the Countess's
Pekingese. When someone suggested he might be available to drive
her and her husband back to Paris he was only too happy to
offer his services. The Chambons were relatives by marriage
to Pierre Laval – their son had married his daughter – and no one
was likely to take an interest in their chauffeur when they crossed

* Robert was made a chevalier of the *Legion d'Honneur* in the field.
† His later *nom de guerre* was *Denis*.

into the occupied zone en route to the capital.

Hensen, the Vichy correspondent of the American Hearst Newspaper Group, became quite chatty.

'So you're going to Paris. Well, I shouldn't worry. Things are stable there. Germany is going to win this war; you'll see.'

Not if Jacques Robert has anything to do with it, thought the ex-tank captain.

Robert's decision to accompany Pierre d'Harcourt to Honfleur had been made on the spur of the moment. Having joined in the affair he would help to see it through even though he agreed with d'Autrevaux that they should be concerned with their own specific tasks.

These were the early days of the Resistance. People were experimenting and learning. Not all of them realized they had joined a school of bitter experience where gross mistakes might go undetected but a slip could lead to a disaster. It was a period when people were getting to know their friends – they hoped. A great deal of checking was going on.

Broad became caught up in the efforts of his contacts to establish a genuine link with London. Two people claimed they could get messages back and he was introduced to both. One even implied he was British and Broad sat in on a meeting in a flat when the man addressed a small meeting. There seemed little doubt that the speaker was genuine in his anti-Nazi sentiments but Broad had to report that he was certainly not a native Briton.*

Madame Mathilde Carré,† who was working with a Polish group, also claimed to have means of communicating with London. She did not impress Broad. Slim, with obviously dyed hair, she had the air not to put too fine a point upon it – of a tart. Her clothes were grubby and her hands not too clean. Broad gathered she was the mistress of the head of the Polish group. None of these factors in themselves were a handicap to a patriot, but there was some indefinable thing in the woman's eyes he did not like. Though young, she could have passed as an ageing actress. He did not trust her and nothing came of her promise to make contact with Britain.

Intrigue flourished everywhere. Broad took part in a meeting in the Colisée Café when a plan to assassinate Laval was considered. Bourges-

---

* John Pierre Wildy, a Czech, shot as a hostage in January, 1942.
† Alias Micheline, alias Victoire, alias The Cat. See page 173.

Maunoury, a future prime minister of France, was among the plotters. Absorbed in their discussion as they left, the group was walking up the Champs Élysées when Jacques Robert realized that incriminating papers had been left on the table. He hurried back. When he returned it was to report that a waiter had simply scooped up the documents and dumped them in the cloakroom without so much as a glance.

Even trivial incidents could be dangerous.

Jacqueline de Broglie's impetuosity led to a touchy situation near the Madeleine when she urged Broad to cross the road and they were stopped by an officious gendarme for 'jay walking'. The gendarme asked for 'papers' and as the Princess argued, Broad caught the man's eye and shook his head as if to say 'Women!' The policeman nodded understandingly and Broad wandered on. He didn't have any papers to show.

Subsequently Jacqueline de Broglie introduced Broad to Steele Powers, a pro-British American journalist who had run an American field ambulance during the 1940 campaign. Powers had a suite in the Hotel Bristol which was a favourite haunt of Americans and Broad was happy to pass himself off as one. He was given a letter stating that he was one of Powers's drivers, though it was of doubtful practical use.

An air of confidence was his best asset, he decided, and he took heart from the smaller signs of growing opposition to the German occupation. Student demonstrators had been fired on in November, the rector dismissed and the university closed. Now Broad saw students marching down a main street behind a leader who carried two long poles. From time to time he would stop and raise them while his followers shouted '*Vive!*' Someone explained that one French word for pole was '*gaulle*'. By raising two (*deux*) they were actually shouting '*Vive de Gaulle*'.

Students also parodied German officers who wore ceremonial daggers. They dangled bicycle pumps from their waists and when the Germans hung up their belts and daggers in cafés they draped their own shabby belts with the pumps next to them.

The viciousness of later days was not then so apparent. A sustained attempt was made by the Nazis and their supporters to encourage 'business as usual'. German troops looked on leave in Paris as a great treat. Had not the publisher of one collaborationist journal proclaimed the future of the capital as 'The Pleasure Resort and the Brothel of Europe'?

Dining in a smart restaurant with Jacqueline de Broglie, Broad was fascinated by a German officer who seemed the archetypal Prussian – more than six feet tall, cropped hair, monocle, duelling scar, immaculate tunic, breeches and boots. The Princess, a talented artist, drew a caricature of him on the back of her menu and sent it over. The German beamed, rose to his feet, clicked his heels and bowed. Broad smiled thinly and nodded back.

By nature Jacqueline de Broglie was mischievous. When Broad was introduced to Prince Jean de Caraman Chimay in the Ritz Bar he noticed he was wearing a British regimental tie. The Prince spoke earnestly of his pro-British sentiments.

'Right, let us all speak English,' said the Princess in English.

Prince Jean was not so enthusiastic after that.

Fortunately she did not tempt fate the night Broad saw Marshal Goering. They had gone to eat at Maxim's on the strength of a loan from one of d'Harcourt's aristocratic relations. Broad wished to return some of the hospitality he had enjoyed and the famous restaurant in the Rue Royale seemed as safe as anywhere. At least the Princess would be known there.

War or no war the cuisine was impeccable. Yet Broad sensed an air of unease. The staff were attentive but their minds were elsewhere. He realized that two stony-faced civilians in long leather coats – certainly not waiting for a table – were standing near the door scanning the customers. When their eyes switched to him he forced himself to nod and smile at his companion, until the cold gaze shifted. Soon afterwards Goering entered with a group of exuberant Luftwaffe officers. Broad recalled hearing that the Reichmarschal's private train was parked in a tunnel at St Cloud, which made an excellent air raid shelter. Maxim's was an obvious place for a gourmet of Goering's calibre.

Broad did not think much of the Nazi's powder-blue uniform and considered it bad form for him to enter the dining-room flourishing his baton, which he placed on the table among the glasses.

Pleasant as it was, the high life could not last. An escape plan had to be made. As all attempts to make contact with Britain had failed, it was decided that the Seaforths should move to the Unoccupied Zone via Paris. A number of potential hide-outs were earmarked where they could wait, ready to catch a train to the demarcation line. From there it was expected that they would make the passage on foot.

With this news Broad returned to Honfleur. He was welcomed with tears by Marie-Thérèse Turgis and with undisguised relief by Sergeant Chalmers. They had heard nothing of him since his departure and had feared the worst. Just what the Jocks would have done had he failed to return he could not imagine. Previously he had put them through a test, telling each man to imagine that he, Broad, had disappeared for some reason and that each was left with 500 francs. What would they do? There was hardly one practical suggestion forthcoming. This lack of initiative Broad found quite disquieting.

Pierre d'Harcourt and Jacques Robert arrived in Honfleur at the beginning of February bringing with them a third man.

André Postal-Vinay, one of the country's influential administrators known as *inspecteurs des finances*, was beginning to wonder what he had let himself in for. The previous October he had been suffering from acute frustration. The atmosphere in Paris - '*hitlero-pétineuse*' was the phrase in use – had become unbearable. He had considered trying to reach Britain via Spain but did not relish the possibility of ending up in one of Franco's gaols. Having escaped from a prisoner-of-war camp earlier in the year he did not intend to enter another if he could avoid it. Surely, he reasoned, there must be agents of the Free French operating somewhere in the country. But how did one enter this mysterious world? He applied himself half-heartedly to his job training a group of candidates for the inspectorate. In the language of the service he was a '*Chef d'écurie*' – perhaps best translated as in racing language as 'Head Lad', with responsibility for fifteen '*poulains*' or colts. The phone rang.

'Hello, André. Henry here!'

Postel-Vinay brightened up. Henry Bizot, a fellow-*inspecteur*, was an 'original', cheerful, open and energetic.

'I want to recommend a candidate for your stable. Pierre d'Harcourt. I don't want him to see anyone else, just you and you alone.'

'If you say so.'

'He's not exactly the classic type.'

With Henry that could mean anything!

'But he has something to say to you. You can trust him completely, absolutely completely. Just remember old chap, don't do anything stupid.'

Henry hung up. Even for him it was a strange phone call.

Pierre d'Harcourt called on Postel-Vinay at his home. The drawing room was large, with three magnificent windows. The view on to the Place Vauban and the great dome of Les Invalides had been the pride of Postel-Vinay's mother. Now, framed by the huge central window, the scene was not so inspiring. Lines of coaches were disgorging squads of German soldiers, leave parties making their obligatory visit to Napoleon's Tomb.

To Postel-Vinay the tourists-to-order resembled mournful sleep-walkers reacting automatically to some hypnotic influence. The gloomy, amorphous groups had been arriving non-stop for two months or more.

'Henry Bizot told me to come to see you. He says I can trust you completely. I will talk to you frankly, then, on the understanding that you will keep what I tell you strictly secret. *D'accord?*'

'*D'accord.*'

The face – interesting. Hollow cheeks, high cheekbones slightly flushed; pale eyes peering from behind thick lenses; an expression at the same time crafty and good-natured; with the sharp nose and prominent brow, the overall impression of a fox. Under the long thin face, a long thin body in a sombre suit.

'Your stable interests me but not your tuition.'

Postel-Vinay found his visitor's smile infectious.

'I am a member of an intelligence section which has been formed within the Army's 5eme Bureau. But it works on its own. It is totally autonomous. To put it plainly, I work for the English.'

A pause.

'You will appreciate that I need to have another activity as cover. It seems to me, as I have a degree, that I could enrol as a candidate for the inspectorate. Only I will have to have an understanding boss. One who accepts a ghost pupil who rarely appears and who does next to no work.'

Definitely not the classic type.

'Are you prepared to be my boss?'

The pale eyes twinkled in the fox's mask.

'Of course. But is this organization genuine? Do you really believe they are working for the English?'

'It's quite genuine, I assure you. I know some of the bosses. There is no doubt about their intentions.'

'If that really is the case I am prepared not only to take you into my stable, I am ready to join yours.'

Postel-Vinay's throat went a little dry at this point. He had been seeking a way of continuing the war against the Germans and it had appeared out of the blue.

'Happy those who have no imagination,' he thought as he showed d'Harcourt out.

*

The Jocks assembled at Marité's the evening before they were due to leave Honfleur. The plan was explained to them, their appearance was checked, and various contingency plans and emergency actions discussed. Broad even trimmed the hair of one or two of the less well kempt of his brood. It was a task he had performed throughout their concealment. He'd begun to rather admire his handiwork.

The men from the Lusts gave him some cause for concern. Their confinement had left them pale and they were not as fit as the others. All were cheerful enough, however, and excited at the adventure that lay ahead. No one seemed even to consider failure. Raymond Lecesne, who was coming with them, was the most silent. He had never left Honfleur in his life.

The preparations complete, Broad joined the trio from Paris at the Bois Normand that night. He used the ladder route to join a lively party. What the Germans made of the non-stop gramophone music no one ever discovered. But there was increasing noise as the Athol Brose à la Honfleur, concocted from brandy and cream, took effect.

Nicole and her sister danced with everyone present and the mistress of the house, normally cast in the role of grande dame, completed the evening by performing a fandango on the table and falling off.

The evening at the Manoir du Parc passed more soberly. The Jocks were fascinated by the prospect of seeing Paris, an excursion which Private Thompson pointed out would have cost a fortune in peace-time.

Some fell asleep early but Dodd and Drayton went over for the hundredth time the manner in which Frenchmen were supposed to walk and talk. It was a practice which Broad had instigated. In their eyes the natives waved their arms, turned in their toes slightly, and were forever raising their faces to the sky and remarking '*Comment?*', '*Quoi?*' and '*Alors!*' French footwear they considered to be generally scruffy. The two big men had learned this to their cost when, having whiled away an afternoon 'bulling' their shoes, they were told by Broad to get them dirty again.

Both had great faith in the black berets which had been found for them.

The little groups assembled quietly in the darkness of a cold winter's morning. They moved separately along the Côte de Grâce, past the chapel in the trees and down the steep cobbled streets into the town. Turner caused some concern by fainting and they feared for the condition of his heart, but he recovered and pressed on, someone carrying his small bundle of belongings for him.

Pierre d'Harcourt had obtained the tickets and the men simply had to keep their eyes on their escorts. It helped that Honfleur was the terminus of the branch line. They had plenty of time to find places in separate carriages. The sisters from the Bois Normand, Nicole with one arm in a sling, waved as the train steamed off. Then they made the climb back to the house and Khaki once again attempted to worry the trousers of a German sentry at the gun position on the green.

In the strangely quiet Manoir du Parc, Marité began to prepare the morning meal for her Briards – she had threatened to leave them all to Broad in her will – and at the farm on the Côte Maria Lust got on with the milking. She had been in tears when her three soldiers left. She had once told Madame Bailleul that if the Germans captured them they would have to shoot her too.

For Gustave Lust the day was one of intense relief. Until the soldiers finally left he had not fully realized the strain under which he had been living. He had literally feared for the lives of his family every single moment. '*Quelques jours*,' that was what the Commissaire had said. Those 'few days' had been the longest six months in his 41 years.

Only one slightly sour note attended the departure. Though the Commissaire had been given the task of disposing of the Jocks' rifles – the bolts went one way, the barrels and stocks disappeared in tarpaulins down a well – no one actually told him exactly when they were leaving. There had been some coolness between the police chief and the mistress of the Bois Normand which may have contributed to the omission. Broad felt unhappy about it, though it did not matter too much. One of Bailleul's men was making a routine check on the train that morning and reported the departure; he claimed that at least one of the Jocks was wearing British Army boots, taken probably from the cache of abandoned stores.

Bailleul shrugged his shoulders. He was well aware that the threat hanging over the town would not vanish with the rear light of the departing train. It might be days or months before word came back about the fate of the fugitives. Until definite news of the success of the escape was received they would be vulnerable. Everyone who had been in the plot would have to be doubly careful.

It was probably as well that the Seaforths left when they did. The Germans were not entirely without suspicion that something was going on. At the end of the year they had finally taken action against the Mother Superior, requiring her to be interned at Besançon. The benefits of her bi-lingual skills were missed, the invaluable rapport with Bailleul broken. On the night after the departure Soeur Marie-Gabriel waited until it was dark, then slipped into the convent garden with a spade and a wheelbarrow and buried an iron trunk containing Broad's revolver and some of his papers. Two days later she entered Carmel at Bourges. The Mayor, Monsieur Duchêne, had warned her that she was on a list of hostages and would be among the first to be shot in Honfleur if Resistance activities provoked German reprisals.

XVI

Afternoon Matinée

'Who are these men? What are they doing here? What is going on? I demand to know.'

Pierre d'Harcourt took a deep breath and began to explain. Things seemed to be going terribly wrong.

'British soldiers! Here! You must be mad.'

His cousin began to sound quite hysterical. Yet the plan had seemed perfect to begin with. The flat belonged to an uncle who had been killed during the 1940 campaign. It was large, well furnished, unoccupied and handy for the Gare St Lazare. The idea was to keep the men there until such time as arrangements were made for their journey to the border. No one had expected the uncle's daughter to turn up.

She had unlocked the door of the flat expecting to enter the silence of her dead father's home, only to be confronted with a group of men most of whom even the imperturbable Jacques Robert had to admit were 'very rough'.

There had been enough problems on the journey. After months of restricted movement, the Jocks were fascinated to discover the world at large still existed. At Pont L'Évèque and Lisieux where they had to change trains they had wandered among German soldiers on the platforms staring wide-eyed at posters and at people.

Even the entry to the flat had been alarming. As they tiptoed in someone knocked over and shattered a giant Chinese vase in the unlit hall.

Having installed the men in the flat Broad and d'Harcourt sought food for them, which meant a lot of walking. Twice they felt sure they were being followed and took steps to throw off their pursuers, real or imaginary. It was tiring but they could take no risks. The sudden appearance of the distraught girl cousin after they returned to the flat was the last straw. Other arrangements would have to be made quickly. As the soldiers could not possibly remain where they were they were told they could go to the pictures. André Postel-Vinay, the quiet 29-year-old *inspecteur des finances*, would remain with them while d'Harcourt and Broad went in search of new hide-outs.

Postel-Vinay, a cultured product of the Lycée Buffon, was fond of good music and intelligent films. Neither was to be found in the cinema in the Rue Royale, which was packed with Germans. Pocket battleships and U-boats, all with Kriegsmarine swastika flags streaming from their halyards, surged across the screen. In his own words: 'It was a stupid film, glorifying in heroically comic terms the German Navy. We sat through two complete performances, looking and listening, because there was special theme music . . . and what music! I could still sing the principal refrain.'

Postel-Vinay's audio-visual ordeal came to an end when Pierre d'Harcourt sidled up to his elbow. After a certain amount of nudging, the Jocks made their way to the foyer and trooped into the street after their guides. It was with a certain amount of dread that they entered the Metro.

Private Dodd, for one, had never been in an underground train. The experience was new, the carriage was full of Germans, and he felt trapped. Sitting next to Drayton he tried to look as French as he could and began to understand the real meaning of the word claustrophobia.

He began to sweat profusely, and as his eyes darted about the carriage he saw that several people were looking at him. At each station he had to summon up all his will-power not to leap to his feet, push through the passengers and jump on to the platform. To make matters worse, at one point during the journey a German private came to sit next to him while his colleagues stood in a semi-circle so that, apart from Drayton on his left, he was surrounded by German soldiers. He hung his head, shut his eyes and pretended to be asleep – not to avoid the possibility of the Germans speaking to him, but rather to remove himself from his ordeal.

The journey seemed to go on and on and did not end until they reached the terminus, Pont de Sèvres. With great relief the Scots gulped down the fresh evening air and set out through the darkened streets. A long walk followed into the heart of Sèvres, the suburb on the Paris–Versailles road famous for its china and its ceramics museum.

According to Pierre d'Harcourt there was, it appeared, a house which had a large cellar, the door of which was never locked. How he knew the intimate details of someone else's home Postel-Vinay never learned, but it may have been that d'Harcourt was a friend of the family. Be that as it may, he had not told the occupants of the house that they were to have visitors, perhaps with the intention of protecting them should anything untoward happen. He explained that André would have to stay with the Seaforths while Broad and he arranged proper accommodation. Then they would collect them at the Metro first thing in the morning.

There was a wall with a door leading into a garden. This led them to the ever-open door and the Jocks negotiated a ladder and gingerly settled themselves down for the night. It would be pleasant to be able to relate that Postel-Vinay whiled away the hours by relating the legend of Sèvres, how the town had supplied dinner services to Madame de Pompadour and Louis XV. But, as he spoke little English, the night passed in silence, almost; almost, because from time to time the noises of the occupants overhead could be heard; almost, because in trying to make himself comfortable one of the Jocks managed to knock over an iron bucket with a deafening clang. The noises upstairs stopped. The Jocks sat still. Postel-Vinay's brain raced as he tried to think of some excuse for their presence.

'We left the residents in no doubt that we were in the cellar,' he wrote many years later, 'but they judged it more prudent to let us believe the opposite.'

Postel-Vinay and his companions were at the Metro well before the first train arrived. Pierre d'Harcourt was not aboard. The party shuffled furtively. People normally go to the Metro at that time in the morning to catch the first train, not to hang about for the second. So it was with considerable relief that Postel-Vinay saw d'Harcourt on a later train. The redistribution of the Jocks could begin.

Anne Robert, the widowed mother of Jacques, lived in the Rue d'Aumale, 9th Arrondisement. She was incapable of being surprised at anything her son might do and when he arrived with a crowd of British soldiers she did not turn a hair. Chalmers and Thompson stayed with her, making a great hit by tackling the washing up.

The others were split between two other dauntless ladies, Madame Martha Cochin, an old friend of the d'Harcourts, and Madame Denise

Prince André Poniatowski.

Prince Jean de Caraman Chimay.

Comte Pierre de Francqueville with Richard Broad.

The false identity card supplied to Richard Broad by French
Intelligence officers.

Clairouin, who had made a success of translating Dorothy L. Sayers' detective novels. Later there was a further distribution and Dodd was billeted on his own with the family of an architect, a Monsieur Bertrand, who lived near the Arc de Triomphe. Not wishing to waste the opportunity, Dodd persuaded the attractive cook to take him for a stroll after dark. Feeling terribly aristocratic in a pair of boots supplied by Pierre d'Harcourt – 'the sort an ordinary man would not buy in a lifetime' – he strolled arm in arm with the cook past the German secret police headquarters in the Avenue Foch. Afterwards he decided it might be wiser not to tell Broad.

Broad, too, had accommodation problems. He had counted on being able to stay in Betty 'Boop's' flat in the hostel at Neuilly but made the mistake of telling Lanova the truth about his identity after spending one night there and received his marching orders. This presented a pretty problem.

Pierre d'Harcourt's family home in the Rue de l'Université was much too hot a place to be used, otherwise d'Harcourt would be using it himself instead of lodging with his uncle, Comte Bernard de Francqueville. Broad called in at the Rue de l'Université briefly and met Pierre's father, a distinguished veteran of the First World War on whose head the Nazis had placed a price. His views on their system were well known. The old soldier had escaped from the Germans in the 1914–18 war by swimming a river with a bullet in his shoulder and was uncompromising in his attitude. His presence in his own home was fleeting. He had merely emerged from hiding to attend a funeral.

Broad turned once again to the American-dominated Hôtel Bristol where Steele Powers let friends use his suite when he was away on business. This too had snags. More than once Broad returned to the Bristol looking forward to an undisturbed night's rest only to find a note from one of Powers's more amorous friends pinned to the door. 'Please find other accommodation for this evening.' *C'est l'amour.*

Skulking about the streets after dark and after curfew was far from Broad's idea of fun. Things became easier later when Jacqueline de Broglie began to use the suite of an American girl, Toni Cottone, and he was able to find refuge there in an emergency.

He began to learn something about the French temperament. Once Jacqueline de Broglie forgot the rendezvous where she was supposed to take him to meet Jacques Robert. When Broad made some mildly critical comment as they walked along the street she seized his hat (he was wearing a trilby), threw it on the pavement and jumped on it.

Later, when they encountered Robert she had to endure his biting sarcàsm. To all her explanations he replied coldly, '*Naturellement*'. Robert did not approve of women playing at secret agents.

Even Pierre d'Harcourt could be unpredictable. Passers-by in the Champs Élysées were startled one day to see two grown men struggling with each other as a column of German troops goose-stepped towards the Arc de Triomphe. One was trying to pull something from the overcoat of the other. It was just as well that Broad succeeded in restraining his friend. D'Harcourt wished to use the grenade Broad was carrying and hurl it into the midst of the enemy.

It was decided to make the first attempt to cross the demarcation line south of Tours.

Steele Powers, who was very keen to help in the escape of the Seaforths, had spent some time reconnoitring the area and assured Broad the little town of Bléré, not far from the château of Chenonceaux, was the place. Powers himself would go ahead and ensure the coast was clear. It would be a walk-over. There was nothing to it.

Steele Powers's confidence spurred Broad into furious activity. He made haste to provide identity photographs for the false papers it was hoped to provide for the Jocks. An automatic kiosk was found – they were much in demand those days – and the men were collected to make a journey on the Metro.

The same dread of underground journeys afflicted the Seaforths. Thompson lost his ticket and stood forlornly on the wrong side of the barrier until Broad, discovering the party was one short, rushed back and reclaimed him. In his excitement Broad was voluble in English but the ticket collector deigned not to notice.

The photographs were duly taken without difficulty but it turned out to have been a wasted journey. The false papers were not forthcoming. In any case the whole expedition for which they were intended turned out to be a fiasco. According to Powers, once they reached Bléré, it was going to be simply a matter of walking five miles across the border with the chance of running into a German patrol so slight they would be able to do the trip by day. He himself would scout the route to make sure all was well.

Full of hope, the Jocks gathered at the Gare d'Austerlitz one morning to take the next step of the path to freedom. Just about the last person Broad expected to see there was Powers, who was supposed to have gone ahead of them. Be that as it may, there he was, as large as life, if a trifle blue about the chin. The American pulled Broad to one side and whispered dramatically that the station was swarming with Gestapo agents, that Tours (on the route) was full of German troops and that the whole idea was madness.

In the confusion Broad was approached by a stranger, muffled in an overcoat and wearing a soft hat, who whispered to him in English and whom he assumed was a Gestapo man. Pretending not to understand, he treated him with grave suspicion until Pierre d'Harcourt identified him as his uncle, Comte Bernard, who had come along to see if he could help at all. By that time all prospects of the expedition had collapsed. The men had to be extricated from the station and re-established in safe houses. Broad suspected that Powers had never left Paris but had spent the evening acquiring a hangover.

The experience proved one thing – the men would need to be split up into small parties to make the journey. A large group was manifestly unmanageable. This meant finding another escort and in this respect Jacqueline de Broglie was able to help.

Shortly after the fiasco at the Gare d'Austerlitz she invited Broad to join her for dinner at the Berkeley to meet Louis Balzan, a relative of the mayor of Chateauroux, who caused a sensation later in the war by threatening to hang any Allied parachutists dropped in his area. Chateauroux lay in the *Zone Non Occupée*.

Broad was introduced to Balzan as an American and listened avidly as he described how easy it was to cross the demarcation line and how he was going to do so again shortly to visit his wife who was ill. At the coffee stage the Princess leaned over and said archly that this was excellent news as he could take some escaping English soldiers with him.

When Balzan glanced at Broad and said that it was not a very discreet thing to say in front of 'your American friend' she smiled reassuringly.

'Oh, it's all right. He isn't really an American. He's a British officer.'

After that he could hardly say no and Broad and the Princess were invited to discuss matters at Balzan's flat.

The strange values of certain sections of Paris society were driven home forcibly to Broad at this time. He had learned, through Betty O'Neil, the Australian nurse, that Toby Tailyour, the 2nd Seaforths' transport officer, who had driven into St Valery to seek help on the morning of 12 June, was in Val de Grâce prison hospital with a badly smashed arm. Broad made contact and identified himself by sending in a solid gold swizzle stick, a present from one of the partners in his firm, which had caused some comment when produced from his sporran in the Seaforths' mess.

Tailyour declined an invitation to join the escapers. The blinded Lieut-Colonel Mike Ansell, later to become a household name in British showjumping, was also in the hospital and depended on him.

Jacqueline de Broglie then tried to arrange a meeting with Tailyour through the specialist attending him. The doctor sent word that he would be happy not only to arrange a meeting at his surgery (where he would be allowed to take Tailyour for a medical examination) but he would shelter two of Broad's men as well. This gave Broad an opportunity to have Turner's heart checked out and he jumped at the chance.

True to his word the doctor took in the soldiers and when Broad called as arranged he gave an encouraging report on Turner. Tailyour, however, was not present and Broad realized, after being introduced to various female relatives of the doctor, that he and his men were really being shown off as interesting exhibits.

The assembled party had been most disappointed because he had not been accompanied by Jacqueline de Broglie whom they had hoped to meet. He was reminded of the peasants at Fatouville on the first day of the Scots' arrival, the difference being that their curiosity had lacked any element of snobbery. It was years before he kept his appointment with Tailyour.

Broad's own social contacts were not always entirely discreet. On hearing that Francette Joba was in town with two of Nicole's daughters, he tried to arrange a meeting, rather as kindly uncles take prep-school boys out to tea during termtime. Francette would have none of it but she did meet Broad at the home of Maitre Jean Sorel, whose inquisitive sons had discovered the secret of the Manoir du Parc that Christmas. The boys and their father showed great concern for Broad's security. Later the same day by pure coincidence Broad did see Francette and the children on the platform at the Georges Cinq Metro station as his own train pulled out. He automatically waved and Clare waved back. Long afterwards he heard that when questioned by Francette she had hotly denied waving at anyone at all. Although only nine years old her security instinct was good.

Would the same instincts stand the Jocks in good stead when they attempted to cross into unoccupied France?

*

The border between Vichy France and the Occupied Zone started at a point where the Rhône emerges from the Alps and ran for hundreds of miles in a westerly direction before turning south below Tours. From there it continued inland to the Pyrenees, leaving the whole of the Atlantic coast, with its vital naval bases and ports, in German hands. Hitler had been careful to make the armistice terms just bearable and the French still had a powerful fleet at Toulon, though many sailors had been demobilized. The Army had been reduced to 100,000 men, the same strength permitted to the Germans in the Versailles Treaty. Headed by Marshal Pétain, the French State – the *État Français* – had sovereign rights in the 'Free Zone' and the French Empire remained untouched.

Two Frances were developing. In the Occupied Zone they groaned under the weight of Nazi bureaucracy and controls – the departments of Nord and the Pas de Calais were actually administered from Brussels; Alsace and Lorraine had been reclaimed by the Reich; and there was the specially restricted coastal area. The swastika was seen over great buildings in Paris, Tours, Orleans, Dijon, Nantes and Bordeaux and a score of great cities. The mass of the people went hungry. On the other side of the line, in Toulouse, Marseilles, Lyons, Limoges and elsewhere, the population tried to reconcile themselves to prospects of a better life within Europe's New Order. They could be divided into three groups, the smallest of which tried to do all it could to restore French independence and collaborated as little as possible. There was another small group which genuinely believed that collaboration was in France's interest and a third which did not know what to think. Most people were in the ranks of the latter: they tried to get on with their lives as circumstances permitted. Their unwritten motto was 'Wait and see'. They were sometimes referred to as '*attentistes*'. In the Unoccupied Zone people went even hungrier as the land was less fertile and much of it was devoted to vineyards. Whereas in Paris the death rate due to inadequate diet increased by 24 per cent, in Marseilles it rose by more than 50 per cent.

No barbed wire fence or mines marked the boundary between the Zones. A notional no-man's-land two or three hundred yards wide existed but was not generally physically defined.

The 'frontier' followed rivers, roads, streams and other geographical features. Among the ordinary people there was a great deal of ignorance about what went on in the 'other Zone'. Normal mail services were closed and communication was only allowed by stereotyped cards with blanks in which the sender could fill in certain permitted facts (later altered so that ordinary postcards could be used). As even high officials of the Vichy Government sometimes had difficulty in obtaining the essential German *ausweiss* * to cross the border, illegal crossings began from the first day controls were imposed.

Pierre d'Harcourt chose the neighbourhood of La Guerche, a small market town in the Cher department, as the best place for Broad's party to cross. To reach it the escapers would first have to travel to Nevers, an ancient provincial capital, once fortified by Julius Caesar to hold troops, treasure, and hostages.

* German pass.

XVII

Over the Border

'Monsieur, have no fear. I personally will see you through. This line –
it is all in the mind.'

The stout, grimy man filled his glass from a bottle of dubious contents
and leaned across the table.

'I know your money is good. When the money is right all things are
possible. Besides, who is afraid of these Germans? We had them in the
Legion. They are good soldiers, but stupid.'

Pierre de Francqueville, small and neat, listened politely to the old
legionnaire and wondered where he had come from originally. He had
a marked accent.

'Let me tell you, Monsieur, a story about a little campaign in the
Sahara . . .'

There was no alternative but to listen to yet another florid saga; just
as there was no real choice but to accept the fat old braggart as a
passeur.

Francqueville was in La Guerche at the request of his cousin. Pierre
d'Harcourt had furnished him with the addresses of two *passeurs* who
were known as reliable men and told him to find a third. The Scots
would be passing in small groups. He had also supplied the addresses of
two safe houses where the Scots could lie up in readiness for the crossing
and de Francqueville had to check these out while he was confirming
the availability of the *passeurs*.

It had taken some time to find a third man and, having reluctantly
agreed a deal with the boozy old gasbag, he had to find a third safe
house where a couple of Scots could wait to cross the line. As a last

resort he sought the advice of the parish priest. The *curé* directed him to the cottage of an elderly maiden lady who was quite happy to make her home available for the purpose, though clearly the kindly soul had no idea what she was doing. Sometimes he found it hard enough himself.

The night before their departure two of the Jocks were hidden at the de Francqueville home. Though their physique seemed to have suffered from the long confinement, their morale was undamaged and Comte Pierre recorded later: 'They arrived with their pockets bulging with grenades. I persuaded them to part with these and later buried them in the garden.'

As far as the young Count was concerned the train journey south was memorable, not because of incidents but because of the strange atmosphere. It began on a fine morning when his father accompanied the party to the platform to see them off. Comte Bernard bought a couple of newspapers and the Scots were told to bury their heads in them throughout the journey. On no account were they to speak. This point Pierre de Francqueville considered rather academic as, though he believed he spoke good English, he could not decipher a word his charges said. As far as he was concerned they were '*des paysans écossais, assez primitifs qui parlaient un anglais absolument incomprehensible pour moi*'.

From the seat opposite he was hypnotised by the appearance of his travelling companions. They were completely different from all the other passengers. They sat radiating a rosy glow – one of them had shaggy red hair, and was heavily freckled. Frenchmen, fair and dark, blue-eyed and brown-eyed, were distributed throughout the compartment but none bore the slightest resemblance to the fugitives. Every time one of them gazed out of the window de Francqueville was transfixed until he buried his face in the newspaper again. It seemed impossible that they could travel 160 miles without drawing attention to themselves. The thought that at the end of the line he would have to rely on the assistance of a half-witted old woman and a drunken legionnaire made the situation even more incredible.

Pierre de Francqueville had been born at Nevers after the Germans had overrun the family home near Cambrai at the beginning of the First World War. Among his relatives in the area was 'Uncle Hervé', owner of the local newspaper, the '*Bien Publique*', who made sure the caretaker at the printing works had three bicycles waiting for him. On these the trio pedalled sedately through the town, crossed the only bridge over the Loire and then sweated the thirteen miles to La Guerche.

Having been told it was up to the leader of each group of escapers to cross the line as the opportunity arose, de Francqueville wasted no time. As his hairy red companions could hardly trail about with him he led them into a church where he left them in an attitude of prayer. From the church he cycled off to remind the old lady of her promise to take in two visitors and then sought out the legionnaire. The old *passeur* was anchored to a café table drinking steadily. They fixed a firm rendezvous for 10 pm.

Hurrying back to the church, de Francqueville led the soldiers to the old lady's cottage where he left them to be called for – like suitcases at a station. Their phlegmatic acceptance of their role as luggage he found astonishing, their trust touching. Leaving the bemused old lady rustling up a snack for her guests he set out to check the area again and suddenly felt the need for a simple meal and for peace and quiet.

By sheer chance Pierre d'Harcourt was in the local inn and the cousins ate together, but not in peace and quiet. Noise, turmoil, smoke and intrigue surrounded them. All sorts of people packed the place, most of them talking at the tops of their voices. It was obvious to d'Harcourt that they all had the same goal in mind and even his own intentions must have been clear because a charming young woman pleaded with him to take her over the border to join her husband. It took all his willpower to refuse. In the midst of it all a German police-man entered to check papers and, though there were no problems, the visit made him feel uneasy. It was apparent the man was simply checking to see how many people were going to attempt to cross the border that night.

Leaving his cousin, de Francqueville collected his Scots and led them to the rendezvous. Sure enough the legionnaire was waiting, now quite drunk but highly optimistic.

The *passeur* glossed over the fact that, contrary to their agreement, half a dozen others, male and female, had joined the party.

'Trust me, Monsieur. I could take ten times as many over . . . hic! I know every foot of this corner . . . and the German . . . hic . . . routine.'

'And if we stumble on a patrol?'

'Ah, well, that's a problem, but in the Legion we don't worry about little things like that until they happen.'

The signal to start was another explosive hic!

The party spent four hours on the march, sometimes by narrow footpaths, sometimes by woods and sometimes across open fields. From time to time the legionnaire, who led the way, stopped to relieve himself or to listen. At 2 am he brought them to an isolated farm and ushered them into a stable. The cows with which they shared it for the rest of the night took no notice of them.

An hour or two after setting out the next morning the party came upon a French outpost manned by men of the 1st Infantry of the Line, France's premier regiment, historically associated wih the Cambrai region. The officer in charge was actually an acquaintance of de Francqueville.

Farce and frightening reality attended the passage of the other parties across the demarcation line. At the centre of it all was the lank figure of Pierre d'Harcourt. The pseudo-student from the stable of Postel-Vinay travelled to the border in advance of Broad, who remained to mop up in Paris as the Jocks left. Louis Balzan went with him. Various little cameos of d'Harcourt's experiences have survived.

Having concealed three of their charges in a barn for the evening, he and Balzan lay in the same bed in what they hoped was a 'safe house' watching apprehensively as the glare of searchlights threw weird shadows across the room. There had been a lot of cross-border 'business' and the Germans were on the alert.

There was the trip he made with Sergeant Chalmers to call at the Château de Chitry, the home of good friends. They arrived soaked to the skin but were welcomed 'as if it were peacetime'. Both men were given clothes belonging to their host, Comte Jean du Pouget de Nadaillac, while their own dried. He was a stout man and they had difficulty keeping the borrowed trousers decent. Otherwise the visit was a great success. Chalmers was ensconced in the kitchen where he immediately made friends with the cook. Pierre d'Harcourt dined with the family which was entirely committed to the Resistance, father, mother, two sons and two daughters.

Hitches occurred the next day. Arrangements were changed. There was more hanging about than expected and d'Harcourt was at a loss to know what to do with the Jocks. In the end he tagged on to the family mourners at a local funeral. The Jocks followed without a word.

'Inside the church they never took their eyes off me. Like one man they stood up when I stood up, they sat when I sat down, they knelt when I knelt. It was really very funny.'

After Balzan set out to cross the border, d'Harcourt returned to Paris to collect Broad and the remaining Jocks. They had problems en route with two German soldiers who became truculently inquisitive when swilling down liqueurs after breakfast, but managed to avoid a direct clash. Memory being what it is, it is not clear just who formed the last party but there is little doubt that they ate at the Hotel du Paon in Nevers and then travelled to the village of La Chapelle-Hugon (not far from La Guerche) and the Maison Venuat-Valenti where they had the use of a room. The evidence comes from that carefree tourist Private Dodd who, unbeknown to his superiors, collected souvenirs at most places he visited. In his collection is a card from the Paon in the Rue de la Barre, Nevers, boasting of that establishment's comforts:

> *Sa cuisine renommé*
> *Sa bonne cave*
> *Sa bon accueil*
>   [and its]
> *Tribune de voyageurs de commerce*
>   [and]
> *Garage à l'hotel.*

At the Maison Venuat-Valenti he acquired a photogravure view of the café in the undistinguished Rue des Bersillas. Broad became aware of these trophies only forty-four years afterwards and still he turned cold at the thought of his subordinate's naive but glaring breach of security.

He was unaware too of the shock experienced by Madame Vincente, the patronne of the café, when, in the absence of their escorts elsewhere, one group of Jocks held a sing-song, confident they were as good as free. This also came as news for Broad more than forty years later.

The hitches he encountered at the time were perhaps sufficient unto the day. He has a vivid recollection of Pierre d'Harcourt returning to the room they all shared. He had been making an exhaustive reconnaissance and carrying out tedious negotiations with the *passeur*. More than one bottle had been opened during the discussion. When the descendant of marshals and statesmen returned he was cold, weary and wet. Without bothering to remove so much as his hat he threw himself on the bed without a word. Suddenly he sat up, looked round the expectant, eager faces, and uttered a phrase familiar to soldiers second-class everywhere: '. . . . the lot of you!'

The Jocks looked at him with renewed respect.

The café being crowded, the group ate in Madame Vincente's big kitchen the evening they left. A representative from the local *Kommandantur* put his head in but probably only to make a note of the number present. He said *'Bon soir, messieurs'* and left. The knowing smiles and winks that followed this apparition might not have been so hearty had the company been aware of the experiences of some of their comrades who had gone before.

Private Turner had never doubted that he would make it home. He was a staunch Roman Catholic and his faith had been made stronger by his experiences. Providence had answered his prayers during the battles in the north and Our Lady had protected him at Honfleur and during their travels to and from Paris.

There had been tension in the air ever since they left the café. Louis Balzan had been edgy. Bob Osborne had noticed it. The appearance of a mass of civilian refugees had not improved matters.

All had gone well until they reached a field supposed to be on the actual border. Then shadowy figures appeared, dogs barked, whistles blew, lights flashed and the civilians panicked.

'Halte!' Flame shot from the blackness of a hedge. There was nothing to do but join in the general flight.

There were some good soldiers in that German patrol, men who did not fire high like the searchlight detachment they had bumped into after St Valery. Bullets ripped the turf. A tuft of grass shot into the air a few feet in front of Turner and he reeled from a blow on the leg.

If the encounter had occurred some months later the Germans might not have let the fugitives disperse into the *Zone Libre*, but at that time they were still hoping to win friends.

When Turner felt that it was safe to stop he found that a bullet had grazed his thigh. Robert Osborne was not so lucky. A shot had smashed one arm.

The presence of a noisy crowd of civilian refugees on Broad's excursion across the line filled him with apprehension. It seemed impossible that they would not be heard as most of them appeared to be burdened with kitchen utensils.

'If I shout "caberfeidh" run for it,' he told his companions before they set out. 'Just follow me.'

Despite the clinking and clanking, the journey to the border passed uneventfully until a distant clip-clopping was heard – horses' hooves on a metalled surface.

The fugitives were on the side of a thick hedge nearest to the road. There was no way in which they could force their way through it.

They could do nothing but freeze. The pots and pans ceased to rattle. Broad felt his hair prickle as he realized that the three mounted men were accompanied by the same number of soldiers with dogs. But no dogs were unleashed. No horseman turned his head and finally the last clip-clop faded away. Sometime after midnight the fugitives found shelter in a farmhouse.

The next forty-eight hours were highly frustrating for Broad. He had intended to regroup his men in the *Zone Libre* and start arranging their repatriation together, but it quickly became clear that this was going to be difficult, if not impossible. The Seven Dwarfs and their adopted Norman companion, Raymond Lecesne, had been scattered. The men who crossed with Pierre de Francqueville and the two men who had been wounded were already on their way to the south. Somewhere, probably in Marseilles, it was believed that the American consul would handle the details involved in returning them home. Louis Balzan, though unwounded by the bullets which had hit Turner and Osborne, had been too shaken to wait to see what happened next and had retired to his home near Chateauroux. After waiting for a time, de Francqueville had headed south.

At Sancoins and St Amand Mont-Rond, the towns nearest the crossing point, Broad missed other members of his party by a matter of hours. Officials at the gendarmerie at St Amand issued him with a first-class rail ticket and a gendarme as escort and he set off in pursuit of his missing subordinates. The Jocks who were with him got third-class tickets. The distinction made no difference. Officer, Jocks and gendarme had to stand in the corridors all the way to Marseilles.

XVIII
Beau Chumps

Fine city though it might be, Marseilles quickly lost its appeal for Private Dodd. At first the wooded hills forming an imposing amphitheatre for the boulevards and avenues sweeping down to the Mediterranean had impressed him. The gilded Virgin on the towering steeple of Notre Dame de la Garde dominated the town and seemed as welcoming as did the mild spring weather. It had all seemed to be plain sailing until Broad and the gendarme reported to the local military headquarters. There instinct told him something was wrong. No one knew anything about them. They were told they would have to report somewhere else. 'Somewhere else' turned out to be a gaol – or at least a detention barracks. The prisoners, as far as Dodd could make out, were all from the Foreign Legion.

They were in a spartan barrack room which they shared with the legionnaires. Dodd had been fond of the Legion since an exercise on the Belgian coast the previous year. A tent had burned down on a freezing night and they had discovered that the canteen of the Legion battalion next to them was open and still selling rum at 4 am. He was sorry the same facilities were not available at Ste Marthe barracks. The Jocks found themselves back in the army with a vengeance. When an NCO entered they had to leap to attention.

Latrine facilities did not exist. They had to use the prison yard which was swilled down every morning. Anyone who was seen in the yard with his clothes on at night would be shot, they were warned.

To make matters worst the legionnaires did not at all resemble Gary Cooper or the splendid types described by P. C. Wren. They were shifty, hard and light-fingered. Fortunately there were enough British in the barrack-room to enable them to guard their belongings.

Broad was having a frustrating conversation with the commandant of the establishment. He hoped his captor would be sympathetic enough to let him make a phone call to a relative of Pierre d'Harcourt so that he could pass on word of their plight and perhaps secure relief. The commandant would have none of it. If Broad gave him any trouble he would find himself in solitary confinement. Concluding that the commandant was an NCO promoted because no officer from a decent regiment would take a gaoler's job, Broad gave a defiant glare before stalking out. Back in the pungent courtyard he did not feel as confident as he had tried to appear in the commandant's office.

Actually it did not take him long to discover that Ste Marthe had its good points. The most promising was that it was a mixed detention and transit camp. Apart from its constant complement of legionnaires undergoing punishment, there were two types of Allied soldier: those who were, like his own men, able-bodied and potentially capable of fighting again, and those who had been wounded or were recovering from illnesses which made them unlikely to continue active service. The first group was destined for an internment camp, according to international conventions; the second, known as *reformé* prisoners, was awaiting repatriation. Because the latter had nothing to gain by trying to escape they were allowed to visit the city. Passes consisted of pieces of plain paper typed with the relevant words. The next morning Broad waved a piece of blank paper at the Senegalese sentry, shouted a cheerful French phrase or two, and walked out with Private Rankine of the 4th Seaforths, who possessed a genuine pass.

Broad was now free, with a little money, Steele Powers's letter describing him as an American ambulance driver and the address of the head of the firm which made Noilly-Prat, given him by Pierre d'Harcourt. A tram ride took him to the smart suburb where the aperitif king * lived, and where he learned that the family was away on a ski-ing holiday.

Fortunately Rankine proved to be a bright young soldier and was able to tell Broad that a Captain Garrow, of the Glasgow Highlanders, was acting as an unofficial liaison officer for the British troops who

* Comte de Pastré, Château de Montredon.

were regularly turning up in Marseilles. The authorities seemed to have given him semi-approval.

They decided to look for him at Marseilles' St Charles station when the Paris-Lyon-Méditerranée train pulled in that afternoon. In the meantime Broad began to explore Marseilles. He had a scare in a café where he and Rankine had lunch when a smartly dressed stranger who seemed to know Rankine asked him in English what he was doing there but finally the man accepted that he was an American. The questioner, Broad learned, was Baligone, a local police chief who was sympathetic to the Allied cause and was probably not taken in at all.

He then sought help at the American Consulate but, in a very nice way, was advised to give himself up. Instead he booked a room in a small hotel and registered as a United States citizen.

By 4 pm Broad had contacted Garrow* at the station and that evening was enjoying a drink with two other British officers at the bar of the Dorade restaurant.

The situation in Marseilles, Broad learned, was confused and the attitude of the authorities unpredictable. Garrow was tolerated because he was useful in keeping some check on the stragglers from the BEF who were still drifting into the city. Probably more important was the Scottish minister in charge of the Missions to Seamen, the Reverend Donald Caskie,† whose hostel in the Rue de Forbin, leading down to the harbour station, was a rendezvous for birds of passage. Caskie, who had run the Presbyterian church in Neuilly-sur-Seine for five years before the war, had come to Marseilles after the armistice and set up a Seaman's Mission.

A notice on his door solemnly declared that the place was open to 'civilians and seamen only', but a stream of escapers from the services made their way there to seek food, help and advice. The local police conveniently checked the place out at the same time every morning so that men on the run had time to make their getaway.

Other individuals were also helping escapers. Lieutenant Jimmy Langley, a Coldstream Guards officer who had lost part of an arm and was awaiting repatriation as no longer fit for service, was in contact with Garrow.

Sergeant Harry Clayton, a Royal Air Force NCO with a French wife, circulated widely.

* Garrow's organization was the basis of MI9 in France.
† Died in Scotland, 1984.

There were estimated to be some 400 to 500 Allied soldiers held at an isolated internment camp at St Hippolyte du Fort on the slopes of the Cevennes above Perpignan. From time to time escape parties left Marseilles to cross the border into Spain but little was known about their fate. As far as contact with Britain was concerned it was the same old tale that Broad had heard in Paris – it was non-existent.

Garrow, cut off as he was, was trying to 'get his act together' and Broad's arrival was opportune. He had appointed a Captain Murchie of the Royal Army Service Corps to co-ordinate his efforts and that night he turned up at the Dorade.

Broad learned a lot, but did not take to Murchie and decided that he preferred to work with Garrow. Just what they could do was not clear but undoubtedly his contacts with the pro-Allied agents of Vichy intelligence was going to be of value. Once again he felt pulled between the desire to plunge completely into undercover work and his original aim to get his little band of Seaforths home. To do the latter he had first to find out where they were.

Broad's abrupt disappearance from Ste Marthe had not endeared him to the commandant and the Seaforths and a number of other prisoners were promptly sent off to St Hippolyte du Fort. They left in handcuffs but their escorting gendarmes proved to be sympathetic and these were soon removed. At Nîmes, where they were due to spend the night en route, the same obliging escort took them to a café outside the station. It was after 10 pm and there was some good-natured banter with the other customers. A great deal of pro-British sentiment was expressed and finally two girls invited two of the Jocks to go home with them. There was much finger-pointing, chest-tapping and talk of '*chez moi*'. Ever hopeful, two of the party looked at the kindly escort. The French can be understanding in matters of this nature and after some discussion the soldiers gave their word to report back to the station in the morning. (It was just round the corner from where the girls lived.) The smiles on the faces of the gendarmes were almost as broad as those on the faces of the two soldiers when they turned up next day.

St Hippolyte turned out to be a vast improvement on Ste Marthe. It was a proper barracks and the men received rations and money. Passes were issued for the town. Anyone could escape from the barracks; the real problem was getting out of the area. The station was well-guarded and the cross-country route meant dying of exposure on the slopes of Mont Aigoual.

All the Jocks who had set out from Honfleur were now together again. Broad was in Marseilles and so was Raymond Lecesne, who had quietly slipped away when it became clear the soldiers would be detained. The young Norman was a sad figure. Having set off with high hopes of joining the Free French forces, he found himself skulking about the back streets of a great city, living on handouts from Broad. He was also ill.

One of Broad's first acts on escaping from Ste Marthe was to try to get word to Pierre d'Harcourt that the party had run into trouble. The news did not thrill Captain d'Autrevaux in Paris. Nevertheless he gave d'Harcourt permission to investigate.

The Rev Donald Caskie denied all knowledge of Broad when d'Harcourt inquired after him, but he did tip off Broad, who then spent an afternoon searching fruitlessly. The following day Broad bumped into d'Harcourt in the street – their hotels were only 100 yards apart. They planned to travel to Vichy together as soon as possible to seek advice but in the middle of the night Broad received an urgent summons to go to d'Harcourt's hotel where he found his friend writhing in agony with stomach pains. Then, as suddenly as it had begun, the attack passed and they were able to leave according to plan.

The first stop on their journey was Grasse, the perfume manufacturing town in the hills behind Cannes. There they sounded out Prince Casimir Poniatowski, whose brother André had first put d'Harcourt in touch with Broad. Prince Casimir was not at all sure that the Allies were going to come out on the winning side – much as he hoped they would – and felt France might have to make the best of her situation. Generously, if a trifle naïvely, he offered Broad the hospitality of his magnificent château for the duration of the war. Broad politely declined.

Vichy was the next port of call, where Broad was introduced to Prince André, with whom he played a round of golf. The prince was more hopeful about the outcome of the war than his brother.

Vichy's smart Cintra bar was the regular meeting place of the pro-British intelligence world, among them Simoneau,* with a golden swastika in his lapel and a ferocious glare for strangers, and Raoul Beaumaine, an astute Belgian, who masqueraded as a fool. Revelling in his nickname of 'Sir' Raoul, he would enter the bar and say, 'I do hope there is no one from the Gestapo here today. I have something very secret to discuss.'

* See Appendix B.

Vichy, naturally, had its quota of Gestapo agents, but none of them took Beaumaine seriously. He was, in fact, a key figure. Information collected by agents in the field, such as Jacques Robert and Postel-Vinay, went to Simoneau who made sure Beaumaine copied the relevant material and passed it to General Freddy West at the British Legation in Berne. He was never unmasked.

Broad did not automatically receive a warm reception everywhere. Denys Cochin, secretary to a Vichy minister, was horrified to learn that his mother had sheltered two of the Seaforths. He stormed out of the bar threatening to denounce Broad and d'Harcourt. They knew he was bluffing and said confidently that they would have a drink waiting for him when he came back, which he did.*

A threat by an uncle of d'Harcourt had to be taken more seriously. After a journey to visit contacts south of Vichy, he revealed when driving them to the station that he did not approve of their conduct at all and had considered having them arrested, but fortunately blood proved thicker than Vichy water.

Pierre d'Harcourt had to return to Paris after his visit to Marseilles and Vichy. The intelligence bureau had work for him.

Broad was left with mixed feelings. The senior pro-British element he had met in Vichy had made it quite obvious that they would be delighted to employ him but had no particular interest in the fate of his men. After all, they were well housed, well fed and safe. Without the responsibility of looking after them Broad would be able to make an important contribution, perhaps, in the field of contact-making. Though they did not put it so crudely they meant: 'Forget them for the duration. You've better things to do.' Their attitude, however, made Broad more determined than ever to get his Seaforths home. One person would not be going with them, however. On his return to Marseilles Broad discovered that Raymond Lecesne was being harried by the police. With his northern accent he stuck out like a sore thumb and it was only a matter of time before he would be arrested. Broad agreed that he should return to Honfleur and obtained the money for him to make the journey.

---

* Cochin joined General de Gaulle in 1942 and was highly decorated later in the war. He served for a time in the French SAS under the command of Commandant Bourguin.

XIX

Bad Girls Make Good

Broad's credibility and flexibility increased on his return from Vichy. According to the identity card provided by the intelligence service he was 'Richard Brord', a bank employee of French nationality but Canadian birth. His home was given as Paris though he was registered as living in Vichy. The card was stamped by the Commissariat of Police and dated 5 March, 1941. A demobilization certificate recorded his service as a lieutenant in the 80th Infantry Regiment until discharged at La Ferte-Hauterive on 12 September, 1940.

Armed with these credentials he felt confident enough to accept the offer of Jay Allen, the representative of United Press, whom he had met in Vichy, to move into a suite kept permanently available for the reporter at the Hotel Terminus, a luxurious establishment outside Marseilles' St Charles Station. The arrangement was too good to last. His fellow-guests included the German armistice commission members, some of them thinly disguised Gestapo officers. Though he firmly believed that it was probably easier to conceal oneself in the midst of the enemy than on the periphery, it seemed to be tempting providence. If discovered the least that might happen was his imprisonment by the Pétainist authorities. There were ugly rumours, however, that sometimes individuals mysteriously turned up in German hands. He decided to team up with Ian Garrow, and the two men moved into a drab room in a warehouse in the Old Port. It boasted a bed, which they had to share, and a few sticks of furniture.

The owner was a well-known Marseilles businessman whose marriage in 1939 to an Australian journalist twelve years his junior had caused eyebrows to rise. Henry Fiocca was a Catholic while Nancy Wake was a Protestant. Nevertheless the couple settled down and became devoted to each other. In 1940 both did their bit. Henri served as a private soldier and Nancy drove an ambulance which her husband had bought for her. Their contact with Garrow occurred in the period following the armistice when British officers were held on parole in Fort St Jean overlooking Marseilles Harbour. By the time Broad arrived the parole system had been ended and Garrow was at large, co-ordinating escape activities.

As soon as Broad was able to obtain false identity papers for Garrow, they were able to extend their activities. They collected cash from sympathizers such as Louis Nouveau, a prosperous copra merchant and one of the most valuable members of Garrow's organization. They received information from him about German gun positions and defences on the Occupied Zone's coast. And as they plotted means of helping escapers on their way, Broad waited for an opportunity to extricate his own men. The Canadian chargé d'affaires in Vichy had said he might be able to bring in a submarine, once the men were free, and had promised to come to Marseilles to discuss the project, but nothing came of the suggestion. They spent much time sounding out seamen in and around the Old Port, frequenting the bars at the foot of the La Canebière, the street which takes its name from the hemp rope walks of days gone by. In 1941 the Old Port was a labyrinth of steep, dark, narrow streets. It smelled high in summer and sour in winter. Busy with commerce during the day it was the haunt of thieves, pimps, prostitutes and gangsters at night. Broad trod the streets with con- siderable care. The populace were not likely to ask whose side you were on before they cut your throat for the sake of a few francs.

Soon, however, Broad began to doubt the possibility of ever finding an escape route by sea. The submarine idea had simply fizzled out while honest merchant skippers did not seem to exist. They heard tales of men being taken off at dusk, sailing all night, and being landed back in Marseilles the next day. They had already advanced the equivalent of £100 to one captain and did not expect to see him again.

A firm decision to concentrate on the Pyrenees crossing was made after Louis Nouveau, who still had legitimate business contacts in London, sent a guarded message to associates in Mincing Lane which concluded: 'Richard and I send our love to Douglas Broad of the Debenture Corporation.'

As a result Broad's father had consulted the War Office whose sole advice was to tell his son to try returning via Spain. This message was conveyed in a cable to Nouveau: 'For your complaint suggest onions are the best cure'. It took some time for the penny to drop, and in any case the information was hardly original. Everyone knew that people tried to escape over the Pyrenees. What was lacking was knowledge of what happened when they reached Spain. If the War Office didn't know, then they would have to be told.

Sergeant Chalmers was not entirely surprised when he was called from his quarters and told that an officer wanted to see him in a café in St Hippolyte. He had been expecting Broad for some time thanks to Jock Hubbard, another Seaforth NCO, who had made a remarkable one-man journey to Marseilles after St Valery, had brought news of him. They had met at the Seamen's Mission and Broad had sent Chalmers word that he 'had a plan'.

On the face of it Broad's plan was simple. He would hire a lorry. Chalmers would be warned of when it was due and arrange for the men to leave the camp for a rendezvous. They would drive to Nîmes, catch a train to Perpignan, obtain further transport to the border, cross the Pyrenees on foot and go home via Gibraltar.

Had he just left it at that Sergeant Chalmers would have been happy. But Mr Broad wanted to see the men and talk to them. There was nothing a good NCO couldn't look after himself, but he had to interfere.

As instructed Chalmers had the men 'on parade' and they heard Broad's plan. Two things emerged. Turner would be among the escapers only on the understanding that if his heart gave any trouble he would be left behind. Osborne, with his more serious arm injury, was prepared to let one of the other Seaforths in St Hippolyte take his place. Otherwise it would be up to Chalmers to choose additional members of the getaway party which would number about a dozen in all.

Broad slept in the men's quarters that night and departed the next day.

The decision to take a large party over the border followed the successful journey, organized by Garrow and Broad, of a sergeant and five men led by young Andorran guides who had been paid on arrival at the British Consulate in Barcelona.

After receiving a brief letter from the sergeant confirming the arrival of his party in Spain, Broad decided to accompany the next group himself so that he could find out just what did happen and return with the information.

First he obtained the guarantee of the use of the lorry. Next he secured the money to pay the guides. This was forthcoming mainly via the Fioccas.

Nouveau's information about German and Vichy military installations was transferred to slim sheets of paper as things progressed. Sergeant Harry Clayton, who did a lot of running around for Captain Murchie, asked Broad to take with him a private in the 6th Seaforths whom he had been hiding. This meant checking the man out and Broad spent a farcical ten minutes at a street corner rendezvous walking up and down whistling *The Road to the Isles* in front of a dark, burly individual who suddenly came to life and identified himself.

His last evening was fraught with drama. Captain Murchie reported that his flat had been burgled and 700,000 francs stolen. The news was a severe blow to the embryo escape organization. Tom Kenny, another fugitive officer, had managed to obtain the cash from a friend in Cannes as a loan to be repaid by the British Government. It had been handed to the Rev Donald Caskie who had refused to part with it for a time, not having a high opinion of either Murchie or Garrow. Finally he had passed it to Murchie.

Broad felt extremly sorry for the RASC captain, who was genuinely shaken by the loss. Only a few people could have known anything about the money and Broad was not at all surprised when he heard that the pretty cashier at the Dorade had opened a restaurant of her own. She had been a close friend of Murchie's.

Fortunately Broad was already in possession of a large sum for the payment of the guides. He enjoyed a farewell party thrown by Nancy Fiocca at which one of the guests was an English woman, Elizabeth Haden-Guest, who had been interned for a time at Besançon, but had escaped and was waiting for papers to enable her to return to Britain. She expected to catch a train to Madrid quite soon. Wishing to travel light and confident that he would be able to meet her there, Broad asked her to take a number of souvenirs he had collected, plus his asthma apparatus.

The morning after the farewell party looked like being a ghastly anticlimax. Word came that the lorry had been involved in an accident overnight and could not be repaired in time. The Seaforths in St Hippolyte had already been warned of the date and would head for the rendezvous point as arranged. If they waited around too long suspicions might be aroused. Sergeant Clayton then came to the rescue by finding an ancient *gazogène* truck without any sides behind the cab and only a tailboard which seemed to serve little or no purpose. It did, however, boast a grimy grey tarpaulin and under this Broad decided to conceal his troops.

It proved to be a trying day. Accompanied by Clayton and Private Alexander from the 6th Seaforths, Broad reached Nîmes without mishap but there the lorry driver went on strike. He demanded more money and eventually got it. Clayton and Alexander then agreed to wait at Nîmes to try to organize a meal while Broad proceeded to St Hippolyte. The journey proved to be something of a nightmare, the driver, inspired by his increased fee, covering the climbing, twisting road at breakneck speed. Bruised and shaken, Broad climbed out of the cab at the rendezvous but was cheered by the sight of the Jocks whom Chalmers had marshalled in a thicket. He lost little time in getting them aboard and, unwilling to have his men catapulted over the un-guarded sides of the vehicle as it tore round the bends, he insisted that the driver's mate, apparently a close relative, join the fugitives under the tarpaulin for the trip back. This time the journey proved to be much more comfortable. At Nîmes, however, Clayton and Alexander had applied themselves too diligently to the task of finding sustenance and in their tour of various cafés had managed to get very drunk. Clayton was not too much of a problem as he was due to travel back to Marseilles with the lorry but Broad had to make up his mind on the spot whether to allow Alexander to join the party. On the spur of the moment he said 'Yes' and regretted it for the rest of the day. Alexander made himself thoroughly objectionable and shut up only when threat-ened with violence.

A bright spot was the apparent reliability of the guides who were leaning out of the window looking for Broad when their train arrived at Nîmes. Sensibly they split the party in two and kept out of sight at the only place where they had to change trains. Once again the cor-ridors were crowded and it was an exhausted party that reached Per-pignan at four in the morning. They were not best pleased when the owner of the hotel to which their guides led them said there was no room and pushed them into the night.

Skilful as they may have been in the mountains, the Andorrans were lost in Perpignan. To split up meant that one party or another might go astray. To remain together might result in the lot being picked up.

Broad now found himself at the head of a group of fourteen men, two of whom spoke a strange mixture of Catalan and French, one of whom was sulking with an outsize hangover, while the rest shivered in the cold night air.

The opening of a street market brought some relief but the Seaforths still stuck out like a sore thumb. The very business of splitting up to have a cup of coffee in a café, then accounting for everyone again, was wearisome. Broad decided that he would have to try a 'last resort' idea once suggested by Jacqueline de Broglie – find refuge in a brothel. *Maisons de passe*, then legal in France, were ideal for an escaper. No one asked questions – there was no *fichet* to fill in as in a normal hotel. Men used them at all times of the day, paid for the room, took in a girl and then left. One of the Andorrans was despatched to find such a haven.

Madame was pro-British and honoured. With the help of the girls she cooked some excellent omelettes before guiding the soldiers to rooms they could occupy until the evening. There were gentle taps on a number of doors as the day wore on. The girls were pro-British too.

Broad went out like a light and slept until 4.30 in the afternoon. He awoke, horrified, to realize that he had arranged to meet Ian Garrow at an hotel in the town at midday, just to keep him in the picture. Now Garrow would assume that something had gone wrong and that really worried him, though it was too late to do anything about it. The knowledge spoiled the final meal prepared by Madame and her girls before they set out.

The Jocks were stretched out in and around a hut in the mountains. They had been glad to rest while the guides collected food and drink.

The crossing had begun later than expected. Two Citroëns had been expected to take the party to a point within two miles of the border but only one had turned up. The second had developed mechanical trouble and they had to wait for it. The night had been as cold as the previous one and even more exhausting. Small they might be, but the Andorrans, in their black berets and strangely formal black suits, were fit and wiry. It was a scrambling, scraping route for which the Jocks' civilian shoes and clothes were not intended. Towards dawn when they were high in the hills they were told that they had left France and had to be even more wary of Spanish military patrols.

On hearing that they would have to spend the day in the hut most of them threw themselves down and slept until the provisions arrived. Having eaten, they were able to wash in a mountain stream and then tried to sleep off the effect of the heady wine. Most of them felt decidedly under the weather when the trek began again that evening. The aim was to by-pass the town of Figueras. According to information in Marseilles, anyone caught in Figueras was returned to France. Once past there they remained in Spain if caught.

A number of families received unexpected letters one morning in March. They contained standard printed sheets headed 'The Church of Scotland Overseas Department, 121 George Street, Edinburgh'. Certain blanks had been filled in. In each case it told the reader that a husband or son, who until then had been posted 'Missing, believed killed', was alive. The writer was seeking confirmation of identity and asked that they should send by return the rank, number and regiment of the man concerned.

Mrs Dodd contained herself until her husband returned for his midday meal. After a discussion they decided they would pass the information, which was described as 'strictly confidential', on to George's sisters but that no one else, not even his maternal grand-mother, a compulsive gossip, should be told. Mrs Dodd was puzzled to know just what George was up to.

Private Dodd was in fact a stage nearer reaching home, though it would have been hard to convince him of the fact at that moment. The Pyrenees had been crossed without incident and the group had suc-cessfully by-passed Figueras. By following a railway line they had reached a village with a small station where the Andorrans bought tickets and the weary, shivering Jocks hung about waiting for the first workmen's train. Broad had been told that the early morning trains were never searched but he felt uneasy about the interest being shown by a Spanish army officer on the platform.

XX

Hitler's Toothache

A swarthy face under a black three-cornered hat stared down at him; someone was shaking his shoulder. For a moment Dodd did not know where he was. The man was jabbering in a strange back-of-the-throat sort of language as if he were about to spit. He looked a nasty bit of work. Dodd offered his ticket with a sickly smile but it was waved away. Papers! He didn't know the language but he'd been around long enough to know that that was what the man wanted. Dodd patted his chest as if to say they had been in his breast pockets that morning and gave another fatuous smirk. The man jerked his thumb.

McDonagh, gradually emerging from a deep sleep alongside Dodd, blinked and went through the same unconvincing performance. Then, as Dodd moved up the aisle of the crowded coach, he picked up his little bag of belongings and followed.

The faces of the Spanish workmen were impassive but a girl slipped an orange into the nearest pocket of each soldier as he squeezed past. They hardly had time to mutter thanks. Further up the train they were led into a first-class compartment where Broad and the rest of the party were under guard.

Broad had experienced a rude awakening similar to Dodd's some time earlier as the Guardias Civiles made their way down the train. They had held a heated discussion among themselves when the set of knuckledusters emerged from one of his pockets. He could hardly explain they were a token of friendship from Francette Joba, but they had got over their annoyance.

Much of the rest of the journey Broad spent surreptitiously stuffing some 24,000 francs behind and under his seat. Currency smuggling was regarded as a very serious crime, so some carriage cleaner was due for a windfall.

There were still one or two Spaniards in the saloon-type compartment and Broad tried to talk to them in French, asking them to phone the British Consul when they reached Barcelona and say that he and his men had been arrested. The Spaniards were obviously afraid and he put no reliance on their promises. Spain, as far as he was concerned, was an unknown quantity. It might have cheered him up to know that by the spring of 1941 Adolf Hitler was also baffled by the country.

According to the Führer, Spain had no right to opt out of the war, but all attempts to persuade General Franco to join in had resulted only in double talk, evasion, demands and procrastination. After nearly three years of civil war in which Left and Right had butchered one another with ferocious enthusiasm, El Caudillo saw no reason to gamble away his hard-won victory. The country was exhausted. It needed time.

The Führer was well aware that Spain had little cause to love either the French or the British. By March, 1939, nearly half a million ragged Republican soldiers and civilians had fled over the Pyrenees. They had included some of Franco's bitterest opponents. The Spanish fleet (under the Republican flag) had remained interned under French guns at Bizerta, North Africa, and had been released to the new régime only with great reluctance.

Something else which would not be forgotten in a hurry was the strong British and French elements in the International Brigades. Furthermore, it had been at Franco's suggestion that they, the British, Italian, German and Russian governments, had signed a Non-Intervention Pact. While Hitler, Stalin and Mussolini had breached this in Franco's favour, the French had actually supplied fighter aircraft to the Republicans and Britain had done nothing at all. His victory owed nothing to the Western democracies. Now it was his turn to play at being neutral.

Hitler's lightning victory in 1940 had made a great impression on Franco but he showed a marked reluctance to believe in his ultimate success. Britain seemed actually to have done well in the great aerial battles of August and September. He might be persuaded at a price to join in the Axis crusade – there was a slice of France north of the Pyrenees which could be ceded to Spain and some French colonies in

Africa in which he had an interest. Franco put these proposals to Hitler at Hendaye on the Franco-Spanish frontier in October, 1940, knowing full well that the Führer was hoping to persuade Pétain's *État Français* to take a more positive pro-German stance.

Nine hours of talks left the Führer limp. 'Rather than go through that again I would prefer to have three or four of my teeth pulled out,' he told Mussolini.

In December the Germans made further overtures to Franco to allow their troops to pass through Spain to seize Gibraltar. Franco, aware that Mussolini had been humiliated in Greece and was in trouble in the Western Desert, was unable to consent. Two months later Hitler virtually insisted that Franco join the Axis belligerents; his communication coincided, however, with news of another British victory in the desert. Again Franco was unable to agree. Things, he said, had changed. If Spain were to join the war on the side of Germany she would need considerable economic help. The process of rebuilding was proving difficult.

In the spring of 1941 Spain was still suffering from widespread poverty, hunger and a chronic shortage of housing. Prisons and internment camps came low on the list of priorities. Just how low a small group of Seaforth Highlanders was about to discover. As aliens without papers they were liable to be interned in a neutral country, perhaps for years, until arrangements for their repatriation could be made through the usual consular channels. In their case the channels began at the Police Headquarters opposite Barcelona railway station where they were finally deposited with their armed escort.

The group was now broken into two. There was no room to sit in Dodd's cell which smelled of cracked drains. The Spaniards in it were inquisitive and plied the Jocks with questions in Spanish and broken English so that it was impossible to escape their garlic-laden breath. Most looked like petty crooks but a neatly dressed woman of thirty did not fit at all. She was being questioned, it seemed, about some irregularity in her passport. She sighed from time to time and raised her head and her hands as if in disbelief.

The police station lay-out looked to Dodd like something from a film Western. The sides of the cell were solid and whitewashed, with graffiti scrawled in pencil. Bars across the front enabled the inmates to see the corridor beyond and slightly to the sides.

One feature of Spanish cell-life caused the Jocks much amusement and speculation, but to Sergeant Chalmers it was a matter for grave concern. Dodd saw her first, in a cell further down the corridor. Pressing against the bars stood a thick-set, dark girl in a skirt and blouse. She smiled and waved at Dodd, who called over Chalmers. After a few moments a man appeared and was let in by a gaoler. Chalmers's eyes bulged, and he swung round so that his body obscured the view.

Seeing the shock on his face, a fellow-prisoner, a beaming figure in a crumpled suit, explained to the Jocks that the woman was a whore and that the police would have no objections if the soldiers wished to use the lady's services as long as they had the money, and that this was not uncommon in Spanish gaols. Chalmers was disgusted, but the expression on the faces of the others hinted at ambivalence.

Broad was one of nine people in a cell designed for three. The Spanish inmates appeared friendly but a prisoner in the neighbouring cell who spoke some English kept on muttering lugubriously that he was very sorry for them as they would all be shot, which only encouraged Broad to try even harder to get a message to the British Consul. He was helped by a fellow prisoner, the owner of a sports stadium, who had been locked up for making rude remarks about Franco. Through him he was able to persuade a police corporal to make the phone call.

Things began to look up after a young man from the Consulate arrived, took all their names and military details, and promised to have them out within a couple of days. He said he would arrange for food to be sent but declined to relieve Broad of Nouveau's papers. They remained in one of Broad's shoes.

A basket containing fruit and tins of sardines arrived that evening but the following day there was no contact. The morning after that they were all taken for further interrogation – it was described as a trial – fingerprinted, photographed and led handcuffed into a prison van.

Broad's opinion of the British consular service began a long and persistent decline as, in the company of pimps, prostitutes and pickpockets, he was driven through the streets of Barcelona to the Prision Habilitada Palacio Misiones.

On his arrival he met three Royal Air Force sergeant pilots who shared his views. Having made their way to Spain after being shot down over France they too had been picked up by the police. According to them, in twelve days in the Palacio they had received only a small amount of money from the Consulate. This they had spent on the only commodity available in the prison canteen – tinned fish – and as a result had come out in boils. They did not have even a blanket between them. And in the Palacio that was serious.

The place had seen better days and consisted of lofty echoing concrete halls which Broad understood had housed an international trade fair before the war. There were at least two thousand prisoners in Broad's hall alone. It was up to individuals to make their own arrangements for their comfort and those who did not have relatives to supply mattresses and bedding slept on the cement floor and shivered. A dubious fish soup was all that was available for prisoners without cash to use the canteen.

It is doubtful whether Sir Samuel Hoare, Britain's Ambassador to Spain, ever heard of Broad, but the latter did his best to attract attention. The Consulate in Barcelona was startled to receive a highly critical letter from him almost as soon as he had arrived in the Palacio. He drew their attention in sharp terms to what he understood was their duty – the care of His Majesty's subjects unfortunate enough to find themselves in jeopardy outside his domains. Apart from the tone of the letter they were astonished to find enclosed with it Louis Nouveau's report on gun positions on the French coast, the paper still exuding a slight odour of well-worn socks.

An official descended on the Palacio forthwith and asked to speak to Broad. Cautiously, as an interpreter was supposed to listen to all conversations between foreigners, he asked through a grille why these valuable papers had not been sent earlier. Broad explained that one of his colleagues had refused to accept them a few days previously. As a result of the refusal the papers might have been found during the customary search of prisoners at gaol reception. It was only by chance that the British arrivals had not been asked to remove their shoes and socks on this occasion.

A crestfallen visitor left after parting with a small sum of cash for each of the prisoners. Hardly had he time to make his report the next day when another letter arrived from Broad. It complained bitterly about the neglect to send in blankets and asked the Consulate to send food rather than cash.

This conjured up two of the staff who remonstrated with Broad about the tone of his letter to their chief, the Consul-General in Barcelona, who was the equivalent in rank to a major-general. They did, however, promise to send in blankets.

The staff of the Consulate settled down to see what would happen next. It seemed nothing could stop Broad writing, though this was not permitted by prison regulations. They were unaware that he had been befriended by a former player of Barcelona football club, one Accadio Voltas, who, though a prisoner, was employed as an interpreter. Voltas maintained regular contact with the outside world through his mother who visited him daily. It was Senora Voltas who delivered the letters to the Consulate. She also used cash Broad gave her to buy food for the Seaforths, something the Consulate officials had said was impossible.

There is little doubt that all British officials in Spain were under orders to do nothing to upset the Franco régime. Hoare had what Churchill called 'a baffling task'. The consular officials went to some lengths to try to convince Broad of their difficulties but without success. Their claim to be unable to supply food when he, a prisoner, could arrange a supply from the inside, did nothing to raise them in his eyes. Nor did the arrival of a pipe-smoker who said that tobacco was unobtainable in Spain and that the Consulate could not provide cigarettes for the Seaforths. Broad was disgusted and said so. A shouting match ensued and the consular visitor asked the Spanish guard to take Broad back to the prison hall.

Still Broad's letters arrived and he added to the Consulate's discomfiture by taking up the case of a private in the 4th Seaforths who had managed to make his way back to the Belgian frontier after St Valery. Helped by a French girl, he had made his way to the Unoccupied Zone and thence to Spain where the couple had been caught. Now she was in a Spanish women's gaol while he was in the Palacio. The soldier was frantic with worry in case the girl was returned to Occupied France. Eventually Broad's letter persuaded the Consulate to send someone to see the soldier but the outcome was indecisive. Even though the girl was a French national, she had risked her life for a British soldier. If the Consulate could not see that, there was little hope for them, Broad concluded.

Richard Broad, wearing a kilt, on parade in Paris to receive the Légion d'Honneur from General de Gaulle, November 1944.

Winston Churchill, as Warden of the Cinque Ports, attending a post-war parade of a Royal Sussex Territorial Battalion, commanded by Lieutenant-Colonel Richard Broad.

Richard Broad receives the Croix de Guerre from General Koenig, Paris, 1944.

XXI

'Arriba Churchill!'

A man had to have his wits about him in a Spanish gaol. Of that Private Dodd was in no doubt. He had applied his mightily the moment the Jocks arrived and queued up to be inoculated.

Dodd had been frightened at times by shells, bombs and, among other things, the possibility of being burned to death in his lorry. Compared with his dread of catching tuberculosis, however, these battlefield fears paled into insignificance. The campaign against this scourge of industrial Britain had made a great impact on him. He had been told that the ban on spitting in public places was to stop TB germs blowing about when the spittle dried. This knowledge made his captivity intolerable in a country where all men were artists in expectoration. He was most unhappy as he stood waiting to be vaccinated against something or other – just what he was not really sure. Time and again men in the queue indulged noisily in this old-fashioned Spanish custom.

The same syringe was in constant use without being sterilized and he winced. When the frail young man immediately in front of him indulged in a paroxysm of coughing the medical orderly paused for a second, waiting to plunge in the needle. His eyes were on his patient. Smartly Dodd stepped round the coughing man and, rubbing his bared arm, held out his hand to the clerk issuing medical certificates. The man automatically date-stamped a little blue card. He was saved.

It did not take Dodd long to decide that this Spanish gaol was 'a rum place'. Take the roll call. That first morning they hadn't known what to expect. They had all trooped into a great hall and lined up facing a giant picture of General Franco, who seemed to have got a whiff of the latrines judging by his expression.

When the checking off began some guards shouted out numbers for new foreign prisoners. The young and enthusiastic ones added a blow from their rifle butts to encourage their charges to learn Spanish.

The highlight of the proceeding was the entry of the Commandante who climbed into a thing like a pulpit, glared at the assembly and gave an order. The national anthem brayed tinnily from the rusting loud-speakers and the Commandante saluted. Prisoners stood to attention and joined in the singing of the anthem. The guards sang too but were still able to spot back-sliders who were soon induced by blows to join in the spirit of the affair.

At the end of this show of patriotism the whole congregation was required to raise its arms in the Fascist salute and shout '*Arriba España*'.

Sometimes the repertoire was increased by the addition of Falangist songs but the ending remained the same: '*Arriba España! Una! Grande! Libre! FRANCO!*'

Just to show them how *libre* they were the guards thumped anyone short of enthusiasm.

Dodd and the other Jocks got round the irritation of singing someone else's national anthem by making up their own obscene verses which they sang with gusto. For the great cry of 'Franco' they substituted 'Churchill'. It went unnoticed.

In this 'rum place' there were rum goings on. The morning after they arrived an official appeared at roll call and called out numbers. Every ninth man left the ranks and shuffled into line. An officer accompanied by a priest spoke to each man. There were heated words and some prisoners spat at the guards. When the process was completed the officer stood back and waited. Nothing happened and he shrugged his shoulders, giving an order. An NCO bellowed, the prisoners turned and guards led them out of sight. The priest followed.

Not long after they had been dismissed the remaining prisoners stiffened at the sound of a burst of machine-gun fire, followed after an interval by another.

'They were given a chance to go back to their religion,' said an English-speaking doctor, who had fought against Franco. 'Maybe they shoot them anyway.' He went on to explain that they had fought on the Republican side, and perhaps were Communists or anarchists.

Broad, when asked, said the Spaniards were simply solving the overcrowding problem. Not wishing to look on the black side, the

Jocks favoured a theory that the 'chosen few' each morning were simply being moved to another gaol and the shooting was to browbeat those remaining. True, the walls of the exercise yard were pitted with bullet holes, just about the height of a man's chest. Of bloodstains Dodd could see nothing though he looked hard. The ground, stained and dirty, kept its secret.

Another 'rum do' was the arrival of three men from a German U-boat, picked up after their vessel had been lost in the Mediterranean. Most of the Spanish prisoners had been bombed by German planes during the civil war and would not give them floor space. It was Broad who took pity on them and the Seaforths actually finished up protecting their enemies.

It could not be said that the Spaniards did not try to keep the Palacio clean. Twice a day when the prisoners were allowed out into the cramped exercise yard with its pock-marked walls, squads washed out the living quarters with disinfectant. It was a brave gesture. In the Seaforths' block there were only three washbasins and three lavatories for 2,000 men. Sergeant Hubbard, who had joined the escapers at St Hippolyte, went down with dysentery. Broad suffered a severe attack of asthma and badly missed the apparatus he had given to Mrs Haden-Guest. The Spaniards tried to cure him by holding his head over a bucket in which they had mixed boiling water and what he assumed was creosote. They succeeded only in rendering him unconscious. He began to fear he would not be fit enough to accompany the party if it moved to the internment camp from which troops were repatriated. 'Miranda' they called it. It sounded fascinating.

They marched to Barcelona station under a strong guard – a party of Seaforths, Poles, Czechs and Frenchmen. The strain was too much for Hubbard whom Broad, despite the guards, pushed into a urinal so that he could at least have some privacy. The guards were scandalized but with the aid of a Pole who spoke Spanish they agreed that Hubbard and Broad, still weak from his asthma, could travel by tram. A warder accompanied them. At the station the guards allowed the party to buy food for the journey which was expected to take all day. Not until they were well on the way did they learn they were going to Saragossa.

No one was taking any chances on their escaping when they arrived there. Handcuffs were clapped on their wrists and fastened to a long chain. This made it awkward to enter the lorries which took them to the gaol – impressive from the outside, grim and dirty inside. Unchained, they negotiated several flights of iron stairs, stopping now and then while a key turned and someone was pushed into a cell. Dodd and Drayton found themselves sharing with four friendly souls who indicated that they couldn't have chosen a worse prison if they'd tried.

The prison was circular, all cells looking across a yard at the centre of which was a tower, like a spindle in a wheel. Guards with machine-guns occupied various levels of the tower.

The two Jocks eventually came to an agreement about sleeping arrangements. Despite the generous offers of the use of filthy mattresses they preferred the dirty floor and dozed miserably despite the attentions of voracious fleas.

'*La ventana . . . la ventana.*'

Dodd was being dragged and pushed. He tried to struggle as he awoke but the Spaniards seemed to have gone mad.

'*La ventana . . . prisa,*' was what it sounded like. What the heck was a ventana?

Drayton was equally bemused, but as it became evident that no one intended any immediate harm they allowed themselves to be dragged to the window. One of the Spaniards raised his hand and then pushed the soldiers into line with the rest of the inmates.

A searchlight from the tower dazzled them. There was some incomprehensible shouting and then the self-appointed cell leader relaxed. On a lower level a guard manning a machine-gun was calling out another cell number and in seconds the prisoners were at the window ready to be counted.

The party left Saragossa the following morning, after being gathered in a courtyard and chained by wrists and ankles this time. After a short bus journey they were unloaded in a square in the middle of the city. From there they were required to march to the station.

Some of the party tried to make a joke of it, but to Dodd the humiliation touched a nerve. Bystanders stared at the clanking column, each man clutching a miserable parcel of his worldly goods. Children stopped to point and ask questions. Faces peered from tramcars. If anyone felt sympathy it was concealed. They could know nothing of these ragamuffins except that they must be dangerous to be kept in irons.

The party was split into groups of four, still in chains, in an open carriage containing civilians. When a man wanted to use the lavatory he had to take one chained companion with him plus a guard. They became used to performing a crude quadrille to enable the unlockings and refastenings, the coming and goings, to take place. During one of these operations a girl gave Dodd some fruit from a basket. The little kindness cheered him no end. Someone had noticed him. He might be one of four to the rest of the world but to that girl he was one of one. He never saw her again but he never forgot her face.

Saragossa lay in the basin of the Ebro where one of the fiercest battles of the Civil War had been fought. The travellers took a mildly professional interest in the scarred farms and the tumbled sandbags and barbed wire of abandoned outposts as the train climbed out of the plain. They passed patches of dark green groves and peasants working the fields, but more often they gazed out across a stony beige landscape. A blurred blue horizon began to sharpen as they drew nearer the Pyrenees, mountains they had crossed with great hopes.

XXII

A Sergeant's Pride

The noisome camp known as Deposito de Concentration de Miranda del Ebro at least had a military flavour about it. As they marched towards it, freed from their chains, they could see it had been built as a barracks and then fenced in and surrounded by watchtowers to hold prisoners. They prayed that they would not be there very long.

The mood of optimism vanished as they lined up on arrival. A crowd had drifted down to look over the newcomers and they recognized familiar faces, including the sergeant pilots whom they thought would have been repatriated by then.

The group was put through the usual induction procedures and Broad advised Dodd to register himself as Scottish to avoid any questions being asked as to why he, an Englishman, was serving in a Scottish regiment. By contrast he allowed himself to be entered as a French officer as per his false demobilization papers. A frantic shouting from a window drew his attention to Wilkins, one of the little band of officers he had met in Marseilles. He gathered that it was essential to establish that he was commissioned if he did not want to have his head shaved 'for hygiene reasons'. It didn't seem to matter very much at that time whether he was French or British so he did not bother to press the matter of his true nationality.

While he was being dealt with the Jocks were marched off. Dodd watched with grim fascination as the '*barbero*' used hand shears to cut swathes from Sergeant Chalmers's head. The stubble was then roughly soaped and every bristle removed with an open razor. When it came to his turn he shut his eyes.

Turner, who had thick auburn hair, looked in absolute misery and it was a very downcast party which followed a guard to one of the huts. It turned out better than they expected.

They inspected the double tier of bunks which ran up each side of the room. The top beds were all taken but those on the bottom were empty. The Polish prisoners who were already installed made it clear they were welcome to them. In no time they were chatting – all except Turner who sat disconsolately on the side of his bunk.

The ordinary British soldier is a strange animal. If a pal is ill he will move heaven and earth to help him. If he has a domestic problem he will cover for him while he is absent. The Jocks probably realized that Turner was suffering from more than simply the loss of his hair. But in their view he should have tried to hide his despair. To relieve their own feelings as much as anything they began to joke about his appearance. The final straw was when someone said: 'You look just like an electric light bulb.'

The young soldier threw himself face down and burst into great sobs. The pressures of months of privation were being released and the others looked on and felt ashamed. Chalmers shouted at the Jocks to keep quiet and leave the man alone. The incident was not mentioned again.

The Poles turned out to be a cheery crew, obsessed with escape plans. With their country divided between the Germans and the Russians there was no ambassador or consul to try to get them out and they had little to look forward to. The Seaforths thought it was rather decent of them to let them have the lower bunks. Only that night as everyone settled down to delouse himself did they realize that the man on top frequently dropped some of his 'catch' on the prisoner beneath him.

First parade – *Bandera* – was at 8 am and after the now familiar anthem and song session Dodd and Drayton, being bigger than most, pushed their way to the head of the crowd drawing their ration of soup and a loaf. After wolfing it down they elected to try for 'seconds' but were beaten off by a butt-swinging guard who recognized them.

Breaking stones for road-making was the usual task allotted to healthy other ranks but, having tried it, Dodd and his comrade decided it was not for them. They noticed that only men with good shoes were put on the working party and at the next parade they appeared in tattered plimsolls they had scrounged. They were put on cookhouse fatigue.

Drayton sat in front of a large trough full of water fingering a knife. The two potato peelers were in a corrugated iron hut, like a small aeroplane hangar open at each end.

They were feeling that they had found a nice quiet life out of people's way when a lorry drove into the hangar. It slowed down and stopped. Its driver opened the tailboard, let fall an avalanche of potatoes, then climbed into the back to shovel out more. Dodd and Drayton looked at each other.

It was not the only lorry that arrived that day. In the late afternoon Dodd swore they were peeling for the entire Spanish army. They decided to talk to the Poles, who knew the score and might be able to find a way out of their predicament.

The most friendly of the Polish prisoners had a name they couldn't pronounce so they called him Pissofski. His suggestion was not original but it worked. The next day when the potato mountain reached its peak some Poles and Britons started a fight outside the hut to distract the guards. Rifle blows were distributed as order was restored but the stolen potatoes were shared in the hut that night.

There were great rejoicings among the Poles one afternoon when one of their sergeants got clean away, hidden on the back axle of a coach carrying supplies from the British Embassy in Madrid. Another escape was planned soon afterwards.

Dodd's first intimation that it had taken place was the sound of shots about four in the afternoon. There was a lot of shouting and more firing. Later he walked past a body spreadeagled on the barbed wire fence. It was the cheerful Pissofski. The corpse of another man lay on the ground. He was from the same hut.

Broad had an even grimmer view of the end of the escape bid. He saw four Poles pushed into line along the fence. A firing squad was hastily organized but it failed to kill any of them. As the Spaniards appeared to have no more ammunition they attempted to finish off their victims by clubbing them to death. In the end they sent to the commandant for a revolver to give the coup de grace. There were spare top bunks going in Dodd's hut that night but no one had the heart to claim them.

The pride of Sergeant Chalmers was badly dented at Miranda. The rule concerning the use of the latrines at night had been made plain – a man had to remove his trousers and wrap himself in a blanket when he left the hut.

This he regarded as beneath the dignity of a member of the Ser-

geants' Mess of the 2nd Seaforth Highlanders and one evening he
attempted to leave the hut fully clothed. When the guard, who
occupied a small room at the end of the hut, ordered him back
Chalmers started to argue. It was not only humiliating to have to
remove his trousers but it stuck in his craw to have to take orders from
a private soldier. The argument became a row and it could end in only
one way. The soldier battered Chalmers to the floor with the butt of
his rifle and kicked him repeatedly as he lay there. The others were
helpless to intervene. Tough as he was, Jimmy Chalmers had to give
in. Battered and bloody he took off his trousers and staggered into the
night. Some of his comrades thought he had been stupid; some admired
him. The rule remained unchanged.

Broad was now ill again and though he wore an overcoat – a stylish
affair made by a fellow prisoner in the Palacio – during the day he
could not get warm. At night he suffered from a raging temperature. A
cheerful Polish doctor diagnosed typhus which he said usually ended in
death because the victim's heart gave out through exhaustion. Broad
also had other problems. In the camp records he was registered as
French. His fake identity card and demobilization papers were in his
file. If he wanted to get back to Britain he would first have to get his
name included on the list sent to the British Embassy and then retrieve
the damning documents from the file.

The first part was not too difficult but getting hold of the papers
proved to be more of a problem. In the end, with the help of a Spanish-
speaking prisoner who claimed to be an Australian but was believed to
be a Rumanian Jew, one of the clerks was bribed to extract the telltale
documents. A number of prisoners chipped in small amounts of cash
and the rest came from the funds supplied by the British Embassy.

Broad felt easier in his mind after this achievement and his health
began to improve. The four officers with whom he shared a hut had
been dividing his rations and put on a brave face as his appetite
returned. He was able to take on duties now and introduced his old
Honfleur card-cutting system for dividing food sent by the Embassy.
The result was a deputation of thanks from the troops and a red face
for the previous distributor who had been keeping the lion's share for
the officers. As ever, food was the main preoccupation of all prisoners.
Soup was issued twice a day and it was possible to buy one cheese roll
per day at the prison canteen. Sometimes, with the money from the
Embassy, guards could be bribed to bring in food but most of the men
went hungry most of the time.

The claiming of prisoners by the Embassy seemed to follow no dis-
cernable pattern. Some people departed after days, others after weeks.
Broad's party was lucky enough to move on after a fortnight, but they
nearly went without him. The prison officer who had filed away Broad's
original French identity papers could not believe his eyes when he saw
him claimed as a British officer. He was called in and asked to admit
that he was a French officer.

Broad blandly replied that he didn't understand them. Could they
speak English? They couldn't and continued in French.

He did his best to appear to want to help. If they could show him the
papers they were talking about he would tell them if they belonged to
him.

They'd had the papers, they explained, but they couldn't find them.
They knew, however, that he was a French officer. Why didn't he
admit it?

At some point they bound his arms and pushed him into a chair.
The next question was accompanied by a stinging slap in the face.

For eight hours the interrogation went on in the classic manner. One
of the guards would play rough and slap him and cuff him. Then he
would leave and another would play 'Mr Nice' and try to persuade
Broad to tell them what he had done with the papers.

It was almost midnight when he was taken back to his hut. The
questioning next morning followed the same pattern. Three hours later
Broad was cowering in the chair surrounded by four guards when he
heard the dread word *calabozo* mentioned. Now things were really
serious. Solitary confinement could last for as long as the gaolers wanted
and no one undergoing punishment was ever released to join a repatriation party bound for the Embassy. Broad prepared for the worst
and was expecting to be marched off when in walked the prison
commandant. What was going on, he wanted to know.

A long explanation followed in which it was evident that he had
asked to see Broad's papers only to be told they had vanished. In a
blistering tone, the commandant declared that he was surrounded by
fools and that as the British Embassy had claimed Broad as a British
subject they could have him.

'*Vamos*' he told Broad, who did not need telling twice.

XXIII

No Liver, No Chips

It was highly unusual when, instead of the usual coach, two plainclothes
policemen arrived to take a party of eighteen men to Madrid by train.
Broad took the precaution of bribing one of the prison staff to warn the
Embassy by telegram that his group was on its way. Then, having
handed over most of their money to the prisoners staying behind, they
marched to the station. The police were content to leave Broad in
charge of the men during the trip.

The journey in a crowded, slow train lasted all day and was not
helped by an English-speaking priest who insisted that Germany was
going to win the war and that the road between Gibraltar and La
Linea had been destroyed.

When the party arrived at Madrid station Broad attempted to ring
the Embassy but could get no reply. The prisoners were put into vans
and they set off for an unknown destination.

Dodd counted the steps. There were ninety of them and they led to a
great underground hall lined with metal racks which let down to serve
as beds. There were no windows, only electric light. The Seguridad
was a prison for common criminals and its inmates milled aimlessly
around their subterranean dungeon.

Relying on previous experience the new arrivals stuck together and
put a guard on their belongings. One of the Seaforths went off to
explore and came back quickly. He asked Broad to follow him.

Two emaciated figures lay on metal bed racks.

'Hello, sir. Come to get us out, I hope.'

Broad found it hard to believe that he was looking at two Royal Northumberland Fusiliers, a sergeant and a corporal, whom he had last seen when they set off from Marseilles to cross the Pyrenees. Broad asked what had happened, and the men explained that they had got to Barcelona all right, but that all the Consul did was buy them tickets and tell them to catch the train to Madrid. The Spanish police picked them up on the train, and they had been there ever since.

The Seguridad was not the sort of place where prisoners were allowed to buy food. Two bowls of soya bean soup per day was the ration and the two Fusiliers were so weak they could hardly stand. They had heard no more from the Embassy.

Two days later Louis Nouveau's son arrived, having crossed the border in an attempt to join the Free French forces. On reaching the British Embassy in Madrid he had been given some money and told to make his way to Portugal. The Spaniards had picked him up thirty kilometres from the border.

Fortunately young Nouveau was travelling with French Canadian papers and there was every possibility that he could be extricated once Broad could get out. Two days passed in the windowless prison where the staff seemed to be as oppressed as the prisoners and refused all attempts at fraternization. From the outside world – silence. Had the telegram from Miranda ever been sent? Doubts began to grow. Then, on the afternoon of the third day, an official from the Embassy arrived. The telegram had arrived that morning. He had come to claim the party.

It was hard to have to leave behind the Fusiliers and young Nouveau, but at least they would have some hope with friends on the outside.

After being spruced up and given clean clothes at the Embassy, Broad was summoned to the presence of the Military Attaché. His correspondence with the Consulate was on the desk and he was given a severe dressing down for his rudeness to his superiors. An apology was called for. Broad said that he had given the whole matter mature consideration and decided he had done nothing to be sorry for. The Military Attaché, a Colonel, was indignant.

Two days later, as the party left the small hotel where they had been housed, on the strict understanding they would not go outside, the Embassy scored its last victory. Broad was told that if he wanted a sleeping berth on the train to Malaga, he would have to pay for it himself. On principle he refused and, in the end, obtained one through the generosity of Commander Dean RN, who was attached to the US Consulate in Marseilles and insisted on travelling with him.

The date was 15 May, a year almost to the day since serious fighting began on the 51st Division's front on the Maginot Line.

The welcome in Gibraltar was not what any of them had imagined. They were questioned closely in the guardroom by a highly suspicious captain and the atmosphere eased only after a private in the King's Regiment on duty walked over and stared hard.

'It's Doddy, isn't it?'

He had been to school with Dodd.

A number of dreams were steadily shattered after this. Dodd had promised himself a huge plate of liver and chips when he reached Gibraltar. The doctor advised strongly against it. He had to be content with a very light diet. He was also told he would have to keep away from drink for a time.

Sergeant Chalmers had also had a dream. That he would be restored in all his glory as a sergeant in the Seaforths. He got his three stripes on his arm all right when the men were given uniforms at the barracks, but looked with disgust at the hat.

'And what do you call that?'

'A forage cap, Sergeant.'

The storeman was puzzled.

'In the Seaforths we wear Balmorals, laddie. Now get me one.'

But there were none and until Chalmers discovered there was a Black Watch battalion on the Rock he had to be content with the headgear of lesser men.

Broad was found to be suffering from a virulent form of scabies. He had lost nearly all natural resistance to disease and at the doctor's insistence he was moved into hospital where his treatment included calcium injections and a bottle of port and a bottle of burgundy a day. Given permission to catch the same ship home as his men, he had to travel in the sick bay and was fitted out with the blue suit, red tie and white shirt of a military medical patient.

At sea Broad improved but Sergeant Chalmers fell ill. He had ignored the doctor's advice on what to eat and drink and done himself proud in the Sergeants' Mess bar. A high fever caused concern. At times he seemed to be losing his reason and the doctor planned to have him sent straight to hospital when the ship arrived in Britain. This, thought Broad, was about the worst thing that could happen to a family man like Chalmers and got the doctor to agree that the sergeant could be taken home by taxi if the ship docked at Glasgow.

The fever raged and, as Broad held his hand, Chalmers babbled. He was back at The Fort, taking a parade, cursing as he gave fire orders at St Valery. Once he thrashed about reliving the struggle with the sinking raft. Sometimes he rambled about his wife and children.

In his turn Broad jollied Chalmers along in his lucid moments. Always his theme was that they would soon be home. Gradually his temperature fell. Spells of incoherence grew fewer. Chalmers had decided he would make it.

Liverpool was not the first place they would have chosen to land. The troops in Gibraltar had told hair-raising tales about the extent of the bomb damage and as they filed down the gang plank – Chalmers included – they looked for signs of the blitz. There was little to see. The Mersey was as busy as any big commercial river might be expected to be and the haze which hung over the town was due to the thriving war industries. A coach was waiting in the quayside. The driver checked them aboard and peered closely at one of them. Dodd recognized him as an old friend of the family.

They kept together, almost defensively, at Lime Street Station. As the train rolled through the grimy suburbs they tried to pick out evidence of air raids, again with little success. They had been told that delays could drag out the journey for days but as the fields appeared the train picked up speed. Soon they were rattling through the countryside past hutted camps and camouflaged aerodromes. Within four hours of leaving Liverpool they were fighting their way through the crowded platforms at St Pancras.

A harrassed RTO explained to Broad that a lorry was waiting to take them on the next stage of the journey. They climbed aboard and were driven to the Great Central Hotel in Marylebone. An atmosphere of suspicion and mistrust closed in around them. Ordinary soldiers were not normally billeted in hotels, even those under the control of the Army.

The Seaforths did not enjoy their time in London. They were told to stay put, though they were allowed to send telegrams to their families. Though all had experienced heavy bombing during the battle for France they felt exposed and vulnerable when German raiders came over that night.

Britain alone was taking no chances. The legend of the Fifth Column was still strong in the spring of 1941. People were not taken for granted. The Jocks were interrogated the next day by officers who asked strange and sometimes seemingly stupid questions. To men who often had possessed no idea of where they were, who had placed themselves in the hands of strangers with whom they could not communicate, who had allowed themselves to be handled like items of luggage, it was a frustrating experience. The questioners did not seem too different from those they had encountered in Vichy France and Franco's Spain. They began to suspect they might be treated as deserters and court-martialled. Faces assumed deadpan expressions. Cautiously they answered most questions with: 'You'd better speak to our officer.'

When it came to his turn Broad was not amused. His first interrogator was aggressive and sceptical. A row developed when Broad asked that a message should be put out by the BBC announcing that 'Snow White and the Seven Dwarfs' had arrived safely. He was told it could endanger security. This was patently ridiculous and it was not until after the war that Broad discovered that, through the good offices of Sir Desmond Morton, then P.A. to the Prime Minister, the message had indeed been sent and received.

Although the appearance of a second interrogator in the person of Lieutenant Jimmy Langley, the man who had been awaiting repatriation in Marseilles while Broad was there, did much to ease the atmosphere, Broad found the attitude of the debriefers pompous and their questions irritating. The whole affair was dissolving into anticlimax.

The debriefing was concluded in a morning. All were given a clean bill of health by the intelligence branch – they were no longer regarded as spies or traitors. Broad was told he could go home. The Jocks had to report to Fort George.

Though he managed to have lunch with his wife, Broad elected to return to Scotland with his men. He had left Britain in command of No. 13 Platoon and it was as the officer in charge of its survivors that he returned. For months he, Chalmers, Thompson, Turner, McDonagh, Osborne, Drayton, and Dodd from the MT section, had been the 2nd Seaforth Highlanders. It was an achievement unique during the Second World War. Later he was even told that he could have claimed pay as a lieutenant-colonel for the period between the battle of St Valery and the creation of the new battalion, but nothing ever came of this. It was with considerable pride, therefore, that Broad led his little band back to the familiar fortress where they had all started their careers. They were given a rather lukewarm reception and the men were told that the maximum leave granted to other ranks was seven days.

'You will each take fourteen days,' said the irate Broad, 'and I will accept full responsibility.'

Private Dodd arrived in Winsford in the early hours, concerned because he knew the family had moved house and he was not sure where to find them. He need not have worried. The only taxi driver he could find immediately pronounced the magic words, 'It's Doddy, isn't it?' And he knew the way.

It would be nice to be able to record that, like Snow White and the Seven Dwarfs, Broad and his men lived happily ever after. Life is not like that. In the reformed 2nd Seaforths, stationed at Netherdale, Aberdeenshire, no one really knew what to do with them. Broad was posted back to 'C' Company, then commanded by an officer who had remained in Britain during the 1940 campaign. Still a lieutenant, he found it difficult to settle down to regimental duties as he was frequently called to London for further questioning. He had to write an account of his exploits which was published later in 'Army Training Memorandum No. 41'. Appendix D carried the heading: 'He brought his men home'.

His private war with the diplomatic staff having ended, he began a new campaign against the War Office to obtain some recognition for the conduct of his men. He took a poor view of a proposal that he should accept an OBE to 'cover' both his behaviour at St Valery and the escape. Told that to refuse to wear a medal would be insulting to the King, he was allowed no further arguments and the award of the Military Cross, the citation for which referred only to St Valery, was announced later that year. In a private audience at Buckingham Palace the King questioned him closely about his adventures *after* St Valery.

Still Broad's struggle to get some visible award for the Jocks ran into opposition.

'No one really wants to know us,' Dodd told Drayton. 'It makes you wonder why we bothered.'

Drayton agreed and soon afterwards transferred to the Parachute Regiment. He survived the war only to die immediately afterwards of galloping consumption, the disease of which Dodd was so scared.

Broad, too, left the battalion. He was recruited by the Special Operations Executive and took part in clandestine operations in Madagascar,

being slighty wounded at the storming of Diego Suarez. With him
went the irrepressible Thompson. Thompson and Broad served together throughout the rest of the war, being involved in a nasty shoot-
out with Germans after parachuting into France ahead of the
advancing Americans.

Chalmers carried on in the regiment in Britain and died some years
ago, a victim of his old enemy 'the drink'. Yet, alcoholic that he
undoubtedly was, he had never overstepped the mark when on the
run.

The others also soldiered on, though in Dodd's case only for a time.
In that period he did have his moment of glory.

The occasion was an inspection at which the Regimental Sergeant-
Major decided that the troops needed smartening up.

'You will all – and I mean all – get your hair cut! he roared. 'Every
man jack of you.'

At which Dodd, still bearing the hallmark of the barbero of 'Miranda' doubled out of the ranks, whipped off his Balmoral, and shouted,
'What, me too, sir?'

At his inevitable appearance in the Orderly Room the Commanding
Officer managed to keep a straight face only with difficulty and let
Dodd off with a caution on the understanding that he apologized to the
RSM.

Not so funny was the verdict of the specialist who examined Dodd
after his return.

'You are suffering from a severe attack of Wittenberg's disease.'

The name referred to a notorious prisoner-of-war camp of the First
World War from which the occupants had undergone a crippling forced
march.

He was beginning to pay for the long tramp with only rags to
protect his feet in the Brotonne Forest. His soldiering days were
numbered.

The events at St Valery on 12 June, 1940, cast long shadows. Major-
General Victor Fortune remained a prisoner until 1945 when he was
liberated by the Americans. He was knighted and retired from the
army that year.

Not all those taken prisoner with the Seaforths came back. Hugh
Mackenzie, attached from the London Scottish, made an escape bid in
Germany and was thought to have got away. A box containing his
ashes was returned to the prison camp, courtesy of the Gestapo.

Another member of the 'Serious Officers' Club' proved to be a thorough nuisance to his captors. Roland Mourot, the battalion interpreter, made two daring attempts to escape. The first came to grief because his bid for freedom coincided with the successful flight of General Giraud. He was rounded up in the massive search that followed.

The Germans moved him to a much tougher camp near Stettin but he got out of that too. He had been about to throw away some mouldy bread in a battered food parcel from his brother when a friend persuaded him to examine it. Inside were forged papers for a foreign worker employed in Berlin with a permit to return to France. He and his comrade, for whom there were also papers, planned to make for a remote village in Lorraine. They caught the same train, travelling in different carriages. Unfortunately the only place Mourot could find for himself was in the corridor next to the railway police compartment. There was something about his papers which they did not like and he was handed over to the Gestapo at Bayreuth. Mourot finally agreed to confess his real identity if the Gestapo would tell him how they knew his papers were false. It was pointed out that they had been made out by two people – there was just a small difference in some of the handwriting. A post-war check revealed that the person preparing the papers had gone down with influenza and someone else had completed them. Happily the police never made their way along the crowded train to his friend, who arrived safely in Lorraine as planned.

Mourot did not learn of the successful escape of Broad and his men until the war was over.

It also took a long time for the news to filter through to Honfleur. In the meantime the conflict took its unpredictable course. Edmond Bailleul became involved in the rescue of American airmen whom he smuggled south in hearses. He sent innocent picture postcards (postcards were permitted) to relatives working for the Resistance in Paris, discreetly marking them to indicate German strongpoints. The wardrobe in his office had a false back which concealed Sten magazines. Though keeping his freedom of action, he fed information to the local Resistance organization called Group Manuel after a handsome young teacher at the Albert Sorel School.

Resistance activities in Honfleur were not always successful. Once Bailleul received a reliable tip-off that the Germans were going to search the coal depot of the Boucherot brothers for weapons. There was no time to do anything other than dump the guns, concealed under a pile of briquettes, in the basin, but the Germans never arrived. Later, however, they did come for Manuel, who was tried and shot. Bailleul himself was arrested for a time and held at Rouen before being released without any explanation. Equally inexplicably he was switched from Honfleur to Grenoble.

After the Liberation, when he interrogated the Gestapo official who had arrested him, he learned that they had engineered his posting to Grenoble, hoping to follow him when he made new contacts with the Resistance. Bailleul made the contacts, but so carefully that the Germans were none the wiser. After the collapse of Germany he had the satisfaction of heading the police reception committee which greeted Pierre Laval on his return to Paris to face trial and, eventually, execution. The document authorizing the arrest of the former Prime Minister is still in his possession. Somehow its return to the archives was 'overlooked'.*

Bailleul's moment of triumph was bitter-sweet. The other Honfleur police stalwarts, who had served him so faithfully, did not live to see victory.

Too soon after D-Day, Edmond Rouille, his popular uniformed sergeant, fastened on a tricolour armband and, with two detectives, set up a road block. They were seized by SS troops and shot in front of a roadside calvary at Gonneville, just outside Honfleur.

The Bois Normand also had its share of tragedy. Francette Joba married after the Seaforths left, but her husband, Georges Drin, joint founder of *Defense de la France* a Resistance newspaper which later became *France Soir*, was arrested and died a prisoner in Mauthausen concentration camp. She took refuge with Marité Turgis at the Manoir du Parc and, during the fighting which cost Rouille his life, helped wounded Resistance fighters into the Lusts' kitchen for first-aid.

Nicole continued to work for the Resistance and the intelligence service throughout the war, circulating clandestine newspapers. When things became too hot she left her children with the Lusts. The closing months of the conflict found her at Caen where she became a member of the regional council of the Resistance. One of the first Allied servicemen she encountered was the RAMC doctor who had warned her to get away from Trouville hospital in 1940.

Gustav Lust thought his number was up in the summer of 1944 when fifty German soldiers carrying sub-machine-guns and festooned

* Monsieur Bailleul became head of the 3rd Section of the Police Judicaire after the war.

with grenades, surrounded his farmhouse. He was held with a number of other locals in a house on the outskirts of town suspected of possessing a clandestine radio for listening to the BBC. This was true, of course, but the mild-mannered Belgian managed to talk himself out of trouble after eight perilous days.

Madame Morin and her husband suffered a blow of a different sort. Their invaluable plough horses were requisitioned by a German unit and perished in the slaughter at Falaise.

At Fatouville times were hard as Raymond Lecesne was dying of tuberculosis and no longer able to work.

After making his way home from Marseilles he had been forced to work on German defences. Nevertheless, when he learned finally of the safe return to Britain of the Seaforths, he managed to travel to Bourges, where Soeur Marie-Gabriel was living, to tell her it must be safe for her to come back to Honfleur. She did indeed return to her mother convent at Deauville but at the time of the battle of Normandy found herself in charge of half-a-dozen very sick people at Villers-Canivet only six kilometres from Falaise. She and her *grands malades* spent three days on the roads, amid scenes of appalling carnage, before finding shelter in the convent at Sées. She did not see Deauville until September. Then she learned that her mother and every known relative had been injured during the desperate struggle for Caen. The butcher's shop run by her sister, the greengrocer's owned by her brother, and the farms of her uncles and aunts were in ruins. Such was the fate of her birthplace – Villers-Bocage.

XXIV

The Reckoning

The escape of the Seaforths from France taught many lessons. The arrangements for crossing the demarcation line between the two French zones lost their character of improvization. At Nevers a system was devised by an intrepid Monsieur Millien by which the Prefect's car was used, escapers passing over the 'border' under the French flag. But the growing pains of Resistance were agonizing. Nearly every one of the people who had aided Broad and the Seaforths in Paris became either escapers in their turn or were arrested by the authorities.

In July, 1941, at a restaurant in the Bois de Boulogne, Pierre d'Harcourt ate the last good meal he was to enjoy for a very long time. He gave Jacqueline de Broglie an affectionate embrace, shook hands with her boyfriend and ran down the steps of the Porte Maillot metro. Two men with guns were waiting around a corner.

Marched back up the stairs, d'Harcourt made a break for it, leaving his jacket in the hands of his guards. He was able to get rid of incriminating papers in his trouser pocket before a burst of gunfire brought him down. Three bullets hit him, one of which broke his leg, while another pierced a lung.

Condemned to death and held in solitary confinement in Fresnes prison, he was later reprieved through the efforts of his family. The wife of the Hungarian prime minister, a friend of the d'Harcourts, made a personal plea to Hitler, whom she travelled specially to see. The Führer said only that he would not be shot.

Another of the men who had befriended the Seaforths landed in Fresnes – Comte Bernard de Francqueville, whose presence caused

Broad so much concern at the Gare d'Austerlitz. Suspected by the
Gestapo of being a *resistant*, he managed to escape with his wife and
daughter to North Africa (via the *Zone Non-Occupée*), but eventually
returned to Paris and imprudently moved into his old home. The
Gestapo raided the house and arrested him.

Comte Bernard * and Pierre d'Harcourt travelled to a concentration
camp in Germany in the same group of prisoners, all held under the
vicious *Nacht und Nebel* (Night and Fog) law which meant that their
fate was to be kept absolutely secret.

On the same train was Louis Nouveau, the Marseilles copra merchant who had assiduously collected the plans of German coastal
defences. His son, whom Broad had encountered in prison in Madrid,
had by then joined General de Gaulle's forces in Britain. Nouveau
survived Buchenwald but his wife, arrested with him, died in Ravensbruck.

Louis Balzan was another victim of the Gestapo. Despite his experiences on the border, when he ran for his life with Turner and
Osborne, he returned to the fight and eventually fell into the hands of
the enemy. He survived the horrors of a concentration camp but
returned to France broken in health.

The Deuxième Bureau's Paris cell was shattered the same year that
Broad and his men passed through the city. Capitaine d'Autrevaux
was forced into hiding in December and did not reach Vichy until
the spring of 1942. Jacques Robert eventually travelled to England
by Lysander, where he took the name of Jacques Revez, and returned to France in 1942, dropping 'blind' by parachute. After a
series of dramatic adventures he was captured in Nice in May, 1943.
The French police chief who held him was so overawed by his cap-
tive that he joined the plot to free him. Robert broke free from his
guards while being transferred to another part of the city for interrogation. He shot off on the back of a motor-cycle which was waiting
by the kerb. As his escort were making their way back he reappeared
briefly, still on the back of the motor-cycle. Its path had been
blocked and the only escape route open was via the police headquarters. The runaways finally managed to get away seconds before
a train reached a level crossing, leaving their disgusted and irate
pursuers on the other side.

A year later Robert was back in action leading a six-man inter-

---

* Comte Bernard died in Buchenwald. His father had been a civilian prisoner of the
Prussians in 1870.

Allied mission (code-name Bergamotte) in the Creuse as the Germans learned to their cost.*

The third agent who had escorted the Seaforths from Honfleur and sat with the Jocks throughout their cinema excursion was also arrested. The Gestapo picked up André Postel-Vinay in December, 1941. They nearly got Nicole Bouchet de Fareins at the same time. She was about to deliver a message but noticed the dark Citroën outside the house.

'Happy those who have no imagination,' Postel-Vinay had told himself the day he had volunteered to work for the intelligence service. His own imagination was made to work overtime after his arrest. Feigning madness, he was held in the Sainte Anne Asylum, both legs having been broken in a 'crazy' suicide bid. Unnoticed by the nurses, he carefully exercised his limbs and one day in September, 1942, helped himself to a white coat and limped out of the hospital at the tail end of the party of visiting doctors. He reached England and fought on throughout the war.

Ironically the person who betrayed Postel-Vinay was none other than the helpful Sergeant Clayton who had produced a substitute lorry for the St Hippolyte exodus. The sergeant had continued to work for the Marseilles escape line but was captured by the Gestapo in the north of France in the winter of 1941. He turned his hand to the dangerous game of double-agent and survived the Liberation – just about. Clayton, alias 'Paul', alias Harry Cole, was tracked down to a small hotel in Paris, where he had been sheltered by one of his many lady friends. He pulled a gun when the police knocked and Detective Coty took two bullets in the chest before he and his companion shot the renegade dead.

Mathilde Carré, who Broad had instinctively disliked when he met her in Paris, became a prominent figure in an Anglo-Polish Resistance group before falling into enemy hands. She too did a deal with the Gestapo and to this day Broad believes she betrayed Pierre d'Harcourt. Madame Carré, alias Victoire, alias The Cat, became entangled in a tortuous web, reached Britain and spent the rest of the war in detention. On her return to France she was sentenced to death but reprieved.†

Less fortunate were some of the other women in the story. Denise Clairouin, steeped in the fictional exploits of Lord Peter Wimsey, bore

* Jacques Robert's was awarded the British DSO and OBE. The citations for his Croix de Guerre run into double figures.
† She published her memoires *I was The Cat* in 1961.

a charmed life for a time. She fed important railway information * to André Postel-Vinay until his arrest. With her friend Simonne Sainte-Beuve, her girl secretary and her 75-year-old aunt, she continued the struggle. In 1943 she and Simonne disappeared into Ravensbruck never to return.

The Marseilles escape organization which Broad helped to establish ran throughout the war but suffered various misfortunes. Ian Garrow was arrested by the Vichy authorities and sentenced to ten years in prison. Nancy Fiocca organized his escape. She too was held by the police for a time until Albert Guerisse,† the Belgian who had taken over from Garrow, secured her release. Henri Fiocca, whose financial support had been so vital to the escapers, urged his wife to leave the country and promised to join her. Nancy crossed the Pyrenees and reached England but she never saw her husband again. He died in prison in Marseilles in 1943 without having told his captors anything.

Trained by SOE under her maiden name of Wake, Nancy returned to France and won the George Medal for her work with the maquis. She did not hear of Henri's death until after the Liberation.

* Supplied by Engineering Superintendent Lang, a Jew who was arrested in 1941 and died in captivity.

† Major-General Dr Guerisse, GC DSO, was the celebrated 'Lieut-Commander Patrick O'Leary'. He was betrayed in 1943 and survived Dachau.

XXV

Just Call Me 'Sir'

Some forty-five years after the 7th Panzer Division's tanks rattled into St Valery-en-Caux it is worthwhile reflecting on the reasons behind the successful escape of a second-lieutenant, a sergeant and six private soldiers. On the face of it they were trapped. With the sea on one side of them, a major river to their rear and the countryside swarming with enemy troops, the passage of such a uniformed group, each man armed, seems highly improbable.

There had been cases of British soldiers hiding after the retreat from Mons in 1914 but nothing of a similar nature. A trooper from the 11th Hussars actually remained with peasants near Le Cateau for the whole war. In the same neighbourhood a corporal from the same regiment was denounced. The peasant who had befriended him escaped but his wife was given a long gaol sentence by the Germans. For no good reason at all, the corporal was shot.*

Even if the Jocks with Broad had read of these examples it is doubtful if they could have learned much. The main qualities shown by the Hussars were those of stubbornness and the ordinary British regular's basic aversion to surrendering.

Of stubbornness there was no shortage in 1939. Of escape training there was none. Later in the war, as experience accumulated, techniques were developed, especially for air-crew, and men were better informed.

What then did the Jocks have? Primarily they shared a common military background. All but Dodd were from No. 13 Platoon. All had

* See account in *Liaison 1914* by Maj-Gen Sir Edward Spears, Eyre and Spottiswoode, London 1930.

been through the regimental indoctrination of Fort George. All had been similarly trained and this training had been proven in battle. Each knew the others were capable of fighting.

The odd man out was Broad. He was not a regular; he had not been to Sandhurst and did not come from a traditionally military family. He had, however, thrown himself completely into the spirit of Fort George and his civilian background and flexibility was probably the party's greatest asset. Old for a second-lieutenant, at thirty his age was a decided advantage when dealing with the younger Jocks and when he came into contact with mature French civilians. Used to making decisions in the City and to dealing with the upper strata of society, he had plenty of confidence. He stuck to his plan to escape overland when so many of the other survivors of the Seaforths headed for the beach and captivity.

The twelve-day march to Fatouville, first of all across the Caux plain and then over the Seine and through the Brotonne Forest, was testing physically and mentally. Half-way through it, on 17 June, Pétain asked for an armistice. Up to that time any French encountered could be expected to show sympathy to their allies. Afterwards there was no such obligation. Offers to arrange for the Seaforths to surrender were made by mayors and local officials still in a state of shock over the sudden collapse.

When these were indignantly refused – and there may have been some misunderstandings because of Broad's then limited knowledge of the language – no one set the Germans on their trail. Broad's early decision not to steal, or break into places unnecessarily and not to threaten people, may have helped. The Jocks did not provoke hostility.

The exercise of personal self-control as well as corporate discipline stood the party in good stead for a year.

'The men always – but always – called me "Sir",' says Broad, 'and in my presence they always gave Sergeant Chalmers his rank.'

This stubborn adherence of the British other ranks to the traditional service structure persisted even in PoW camps in Germany. A sergeant-major remained a sergeant-major, a sergeant a sergeant and so forth. In the case of the French, all soldiers below officer grade tended to regard themselves as equal once they were captured.

To men like Chalmers the regimental system was the core of their existence. He insisted in preserving it because he knew it worked. In return he served it well. Hard drinker though he was, he did not give way to his weakness during the whole period of the escape.

To the credit of all the Seaforths, none of the people who hid them ever complained of their behaviour or accused them of doing anything dangerous or patently stupid. In Honfleur, where they stayed longest, they made firm friends. Four years after they had left the Côte de Grâce, the soldiers wrote to thank their benefactors. Some paid personal visits.

In the bickering over the Common Market it is fashionable in some British quarters to condemn France as selfish, so it can do no harm to review the risks taken by so many French people, at all levels of society, for the sake of restoring seven riflemen and one officer to the army of the British Empire.

Simple patriotism motivated the ailing Raymond Lecesne who so longed to 'do his bit'. Long after his death in 1945, through Broad's efforts, a headstone was raised to carry the proud statement that he was a *'Resistant du 18 juin, 1940.'* The description 'Snow White and the Seven Dwarfs' and the names of the Seaforths are listed.

Simple patriotism too was behind mild-mannered little 'Monsieur Bloom's' refusal to try to cash after the war any of the do-it-yourself cheques signed by Broad. His house had been destroyed in an air raid, he had endured much, but if he died poor he died proud.

Having experienced the German occupation of Belgium and Northern France in the First World War, Bailleul and Lust knew what they were up against when they came to the aid of the Seaforths. In the spring of 1984 both men were asked if they would do the same again. Bailleul, retired to a village halfway between Bordeaux and Mont-de-Marsan, said 'Probably yes . . . under similar circumstances.' It had all developed so quickly he had little option but to see it through. 'Besides,' he said with a twinkle in his eyes, 'they were Scots and I can trace my ancestry back to Robert Baliol, once King of Scotland.'

Gustav Lust, now a widower, has given up his farm and spoke at the home of Irma, tucked away, coincidentally, on the slopes of the hillside below Fatouville. He was full of praise for the young Scots he had sheltered – Robert Osborne who had tried so hard to speak French, McDonagh who was always *'sans souci'*. They had never caused him a moment's worry by any misbehaviour. Nevertheless their long stay under such restricted conditions had caused him considerable strain. His wife had never been able to leave the farm. She had felt she must always be around. The family had been afraid the whole time. Looking back Lust felt that, in truth, he had been unfair to expose them over such a long period to the possibility of death or deportation. Would *he* do it again? *'Franchement, non!'*

If the men involved in the Broad affair showed deliberate courage, the women seem to have been inspired. Their influence dominates events at Honfleur and emerges time and again afterwards. After Raymond Lecesne first took the Seaforths to the barn in Fatouville, it was his sister who reported their presence to the Mother Superior. It was a bonus point that she was not only English but bilingual, but she had to make a difficult decision. The Church in France had an ambivalent attitude to the Occupation. In Vichy the fear of Communism was fuelled by the presence of hordes of Spanish refugees and the tendency of the bishops was to favour the Right-wing Pétainist *État Français* as a bulwark against the Red menace. Fortunately the Mother Superior took the view that the non-aggression pact between Hitler and Stalin made them equally objectionable and evil. She gave her blessing to all who opposed them.

Confident in their faith, Madame Lecesne and her daughters, Nicole Bouchet de Fareins, Francette Joba, Maria Bailleul, Anna Lust, Ernestine Morin, Soeur Marie-Gabriel and Marie-Thérese Turgis all risked their lives. All knew they were likely to be gaoled or shot if caught sheltering British soldiers. Those who were married stood to lose not only their husbands but be parted from their children for years.

Perhaps, like Soeur Marie-Gabriel who carted the soldiers' arms and uniforms about with her mule, they had reconciled themselves to the likelihood that if the worst came to the worst the end would be quick. The drawn-out horror of life in a concentration camp was then unknown.

Even the small girls involved displayed amazing sang froid – as shown by Claire Bouchet de Fareins' hot denial of having seen Broad on the Metro. Lust's niece, Anna, who was only eight when the Jocks arrived, took the need for secrecy so much to heart that, though reunited with her parents, she did not tell her mother about events at Honfleur until *after* the Liberation.

With the exception of the Princesse de Broglie,* a 'smart young thing,' a more worldly view was taken by the women who allowed their homes to be used as 'safe houses' in Paris. Denise Clairouin can have had no illusions about the possible consequences of what she was doing, nor can Madame Robert, with a more-than-well-informed son, or Madame Cochin, mother of a Vichy government official and a member of one of the richest and best-known families in France. Yet they too accepted the risk. Furthermore, like all those involved, they did so knowing that, if all went well, this junior officer and his seven ordinary

---

* Died of cancer after the war.

soldiers would regain the free world while they remained under Nazi oppression. Not one of them seems to have applied the businesslike equation 'What do we stand to gain – what do we stand to lose?'

The French government awarded the Legion d'Honneur to Mère Marie du St Sacrement in 1952 (at a ceremony in Honfleur attended by Broad).* For the others who helped the Seaforths there was no special recognition and certainly no financial recompense. Broad's home-made cheques were never presented by either prince or peasant. And the British authorities never even offered to pay for the food consumed by the soldiers or to make good the billeting costs normally met. In the 1920s the War Office found a way in which to pay a portion of the allowances due to the private of the 11th Hussars who had been hidden for four years. The Honfleurais were offered nothing.

They shared in general thanks of a kind in the shape of mass-produced pallid certificates acknowledging in stereotyped phraseology that the holders had sheltered or helped escaping Allied servicemen. They were signed by Marshal of the Royal Air Force Lord Tedder, who had been Eisenhower's deputy at Supreme Headquarters. Even these were difficult to obtain, the best resisters being the least conspicuous. Many actions were to pass unnoticed and as late as January, 1954, Edmond Bailleul was writing to Richard Broad asking him to counter-sign an attestation in favour of the Lust family re their wartime conduct.

American recognition of services made a much greater impression on such people as Bailleul, who smuggled US airmen out of Honfleur, and Britain may have missed an opportunity to capitalize on the tremendous fund of goodwill which had been built up. Perhaps even now it is not too late to remedy matters.

In a way this account of a unique wartime escape is a testimony to two disciplines. The Seaforths relied on a regimental system which enabled men to be both proud and obedient. At the same time it required officers to foster that pride and to be responsible and consider-ate. It was a system that in the case of the Seaforths had worked for more than 150 years.

The women of Honfleur, on whom so much depended, found their courage in their religion. Perhaps in tribute to their faith someone some day will arrange for one of Lord Tedder's testimonials to be hung with other tokens of gratitude in the serene little chapel that still houses the statue of Notre Dâme de Grâce.

* Soeur Marie-Gabriel carried the cushion bearing the decoration at the Mother Superior's funeral a few years later.

Appendix A

Order of Battle of the infantry
51st Highland Division 10 May, 1940

152 Brigade   2nd Seaforth Highlanders
               (transferred from 5th Division)
             4th Seaforth Highlanders (TA)
             4th Cameron Highlanders (TA)

153 Brigade   4th Black Watch (TA)
             1st Gordon Highlanders
               (transferred from the 1st Division)
             5th Gordon Highlanders (TA)

154 Brigade   1st Black Watch
               (transferred from the 4th Division)
             7th Argyll and Sutherland Highlanders (TA)
             8th Argyll and Sutherland Highlanders (TA)

Two machine-gun battalions, the 7th Royal Northumberland Fusiliers (TA) and the 1st Middlesex Regiment, plus two pioneer battalions, the 7th Royal Norfolk Regiment (TA) and the 6th Royal Scots Fusiliers (TA), were attached to the 51st Division when it moved to the Saar in April, 1940.

Appendix B

Services Speciaux

Colonel Leon Simoneau, writing to the author from Paris in 1984, states: 'In 1941 I was only a captain in charge of a *poste de recherche* at Vichy. If I was seen from time to time in the Cintra it was because the owner and the barman kept me informed about doubtful customers; that is to say those who believed in the victory of Hitler, or who did not like the English, or even those who were more interested in their own personal affairs rather than the struggle of the Allies.'

Of his friend, Raoul Beaumaine, he writes: 'He was a veteran of the 1914 war, a *mutilé de guerre* and, if I am not mistaken, had married a daughter of a Lord Ramsay. He was the representative for Heidseck Monopole Champagne, Haig whisky and Adet cognac covering Europe, Scandinavia and North America. Because of his personal contacts with the embassies of many countries his services were invaluable, particularly in passing on urgent information to the British.'

With regard to the Seaforths, Colonel Simoneau writes that, though helping escapers was not part of his branch's brief at the time, he remembers providing facilities (eg identity cards) for Pierre d'Harcourt and, in particular, putting him in touch with Commandant Jonglez de Ligne,* head of the counter-espionage service in Marseilles.

After some remarkable successes in obtaining intelligence, Captain d'Autrevaux was detected by the Abwehr, probably because he had made some rash contacts not approved of by the counter-espionage service. He was lucky to escape to the Unoccupied Zone where he had to adopt a false identity.

After the Germans overran the rest of France in November, 1942, Simoneau continued to work against them but took the precaution of changing his base. When he was denounced to the Abwehr in January, 1943, the 'snatch squad' went to an old address. Simoneau went into hiding until ordered to report to Algiers where he arrived via Spain and Gibraltar in May of the same year.

Britain acknowledged his services with the award of the MBE.

* Arrested by the Gestapo, survived concentration camp imprisonment and died after the war.

Readers may have been puzzled by the involvement of members of the Vichy régime's military intelligence services in helping the escape of the Seaforths. The confusion is understandable. However, immediately after the Fall of France, the controllers of the *Services Speciaux de la Défénse Nationale* created a pro-Allied network which they superimposed on the existing structure. They were at great pains to conceal its existence and Colonel Rivet, head of the service, issued a formal order forbidding contacts with agents of France's former allies – while at the same time setting up the organization to do just that.

The harmless *Société d'Entreprise des Travaux Ruraux* (Rural Engineering Works Department) was a cover for the counter-espionage service tasked to neutralize axis agents.

The quaintly named Colonel Perruche (literally translated 'long-tailed parrot' or 'hen parrot' but not a *nom de guerre* in his case) directed the Intelligence Service – *Service de Renseignments* – and was Simoneau's immediate superior. Through officers like d'Autrevaux and his agents, they aimed to use what remained of the pre-1940 *Cinquième Bureau* net to continue the struggle.

Another organization – *Conservation de Matériel* – was engaged in the camouflage and storing of equipment, particularly the arms of the undefeated Army of the Alps which had held the Italian front without difficulty. The stores were to be held until the day when the battle against Hitler and Mussolini could be resumed openly. Some things were done on a large scale – two battalions of medium tanks were hidden in quarries in the Baux region.

As an umbrella to cover all these activities and a number of others, the *Service des Menées Antinationales* – officially required to protect the Army of the Armistice from subversion and espionage – was created.

The main opponents of the pro-Allied camp were the German Armistice Commission with its thinly-disguised quota of Gestapo agents, and various elements in the Vichy police forces. In the complex atmosphere of the times the Army and Air Service officers who worked together against the Axis had to be on their guard also against the head of naval intelligence who, under the influence of the Anglophobe Admiral Darlan, looked on the Axis and the 'Anglo-Saxons' in a similar light.

Colonel Paul Paillole, who was *directeur* of the *Travaux Ruraux*, has written an account of its operations in '*Services Speciaux*' (Editions Robert Laffont). General Henri Navarre is the author of '*Le Service de Renseignments*', Editions Plon, Paris.